D1262569

Getting to Know You!

Social Skills Curriculum for Grades 1 to 3

by
Dennis Hanken, Ed.S.
and
Judith Kennedy, Ed.S.

ISBN No. 0-932796-87-7

Library of Congress Catalog No. 98-72129

Publisher—

Educational Media Corporation®
Box 21311
Minneapolis, MN 55421-0311
(612) 781-0088

Production Editor—

Don L. Sorenson

Graphic Designer—

Earl R. Sorenson

Dedication

This book is dedicated to the researchers and authors who preceded us in the study of social skills and in writing programs to assist with teaching social skills components. This book is also dedicated to the teachers and children who have shown us that our curriculum is effective, fun, and easy to use.

About the Authors

Dennis Hanken and his wife, Wendy, are the parents of three daughters. He has polished his own social skills and developed an awareness of the need for social skills training in his 28 years working with youth in an educational setting. His fellow workers and students enjoy his keen sense of humor, empathy, and enjoyment of life. He is currently a school psychologist in the Rapid City School System in South Dakota.

Judith Kennedy is married and the parent of two children, two stepchildren, a daughter-in-law, and a grandson. A focus of her life has always been to assist children to interact respectfully, live their lives fully, and achieve their potential. She has thirty years experience working with youth and is currently a school psychologist.

Acknowledgments

The authors would like to thank U.S. West and Hasbro Children's Foundation for their financial support which made the research in this publication possible. Our thanks go, as well, to professionals before us from whom we gleaned ideas for our approach to this Social Skills Curriculum. We also thank Marcene Rand, Beth Steen, Wendy Hanken, and LuAnn Mattern for their assistance and creativity.

We thank "Dear Wally" publishers, Guideposts Book Division, 16 East 34th St., New York, NY 10016, for the use of the "Dear Wally" letters to support our curriculum and *Aesop's Fable* which complement our lessons.

Table of Contents

Introduction

Why teach social skills? The question of whether it is the responsibility of schools to teach socially appropriate behavior has been debated for years, but the fact remains that educators are dealing increasingly with maladjusted behavior. According to statistics from the U. S. Department of Education, three to six percent of the school population have significant social adjustment problems. Many students who enter kindergarten come from homes that are dysfunctional, abusive, economically impoverished, or that contain alcohol or drug addicted parents.

More children than ever come from nontraditional families with parents who are underemployed and even in their teens. Professionals report that the decline of the family unit, changing morals, the step-family, drug and alcohol abuse, working parents, television, and rising crime rate are just a few of the things that have caused children to be less proficient in appropriate social behavior. However, even children who benefit from exposure to appropriate social behavior at home, church, or in their communities have a need to learn the parameters of expected behaviors in school.

Teaching social skills helps eliminate problematic behaviors. Educators are then free to teach academics rather than deal with disruptive behaviors. A good social skills curriculum teaches the appropriate behavior rather than correcting the inappropriate behavior. This approach has proven in field studies to decrease inappropriate behavior while increasing the desired behavior.

In the last ten years, social skills research and curriculums have appeared all over the United States. Journal articles have focused on this area. Social skills training programs have become an integral component of special education curricula (Schumaker, Pederson, Hazel, and Meyer, 1983). However, experience has shown that teaching social skills in isolation fails to transfer those skills back to the regular classroom, playground, community, and home (Gresham, 1986). An additional disadvantage to teaching social skills only to children in special education is that it fails to reach other at-risk youth who do not qualify for special education programs.

Who benefits from learning social skills?

- Children who are either withdrawn or aggressive;
- Children who are developing normally, but who have periodic deficits in prosocial skill behaviors;
- Children who have learning disabilities, communication disorders, behavioral problems, or other handicaps (Burstien, 1986). These children tend to interact more with teachers than with peers.

Effective social skills curricula. The authors of this curriculum have researched many books, curricula, and theories on social skills training to identify the ingredients of an effective social curriculum. These ingredients are:

1. Use a proactive approach—teach all students the desired behaviors rather than spend time correcting disruptive behaviors.
2. Teach the curriculum daily just as one does math and reading.
3. Involve all personnel in the school in the curriculum so the desired behavior is reinforced in all environments.
4. Use a common language that all personnel and children identify as steps to the desired behavior.
5. Model and role play each skill component.
6. Involve parents in reinforcing the skills.

The *Getting to Know You* Curriculum. This curriculum is well researched and has each of these ingredients. It has been field tested in schools where it helped decrease maladaptive behaviors by 70% This curriculum can do the same for you. It is designed to be used in the regular classroom where it will benefit all students regardless of race, creed, color, or academic ability. It was developed in a city school system in a rural region with a diverse student population to include a large percentage of Lakota Native Americans and U.S. Air Force families.

The authors believe that social skills can be taught like academics in a positive mode rather than using punishment as a means to control social behavior. This is called a prosocial skills approach and focuses on teaching new skills rather than correcting maladaptive behavior.

Our philosophy is: students come to school with varying levels of social skill development. Research shows that new social skills are best learned by using the components of modeling, role playing, performance feedback, and transfer training. Providing a student with correct strategies and practice to increase performance works for both academics and social skills.

Our component model for the development of social skills is:

Model the skill—the teacher demonstrates "Think Aloud" steps.

Role play with feed back—the students rehearse and practice skill steps with positive feedback and corrections.

Transfer activities—the children will use these newly learned skills in real-life situations.

Our instruction model includes:

Identifying the skill/establishing the need

Identifying situations in which the skill is needed

Presenting the steps of the skill

Modeling the skill (teacher or older students)

"Think Aloud"—internal dialogue or practice in your mind of the skill steps

Guided role playing—practice for students using appropriate role playing of new skill (some authors recommend an additional inappropriate example for teaching purposes)

Positive feedback—corrections

Transfer training to generalize the skill

Maintenance activities

Prosocial skills to be covered in the manual:

I. Classroom Skills

II. Friendship Skills

III. Expressing Feelings

IV. Relieving Stress

V. Making Decisions

VI. Replacement Skills

VII. Self Acceptance

This curriculum has lesson plans for each skill that are easy to implement for the regular classroom teacher. Each lesson contains an objective which states the purpose of the lesson, lists the materials needed, and cites a reason for acquiring the skill. The teacher then models the skill, after which the students practice an appropriate example of the skill. An inappropriate example of the skill is included in "Helpful Hints" to contrast the right and wrong way the skill is done. This format is based on current research which outlines that children learn best when given a model of a behavior and time to practice the skill with feedback.

An important component of this model is transfer training. Many social skills programs fail because they do not provide the student with opportunities to apply the social skill they learned in real-life situations. This model provides homework assignments to be done in other areas of the school, at home or in the community and with peers. Assigning these activities and seeing that they are completed is an integral component of this model, and will make the difference in successful generalization of these skills to other environments.

The end of each lesson contains comments, if needed, and extended activities which can be used if the students have not fully mastered the skill. These are enjoyable activities the students will perform in real life situations to more fully reinforce the learning of these skills.

Some lessons may need to be taught several days so that all students learn the skill, while other lessons may require only one teaching. It will be beneficial to review the previously learned skills in order to ensure mastery.

When you decide as a group or school to use this curriculum, you many want to pick two to four skills to focus on each quarter of the year. Review these skills at the end of the school year. By the time your kindergarten children are in the upper grades, they should be good role models for the younger children in your school.

Our intent is for this curriculum to be easy as well as fun to teach. We hope you and your students enjoy it.

Instructions for Using this Curriculum

1. This curriculum is based on well-researched practices. One of the reasons for its documented success is the "Think Aloud" strategies. These strategies are actually the internal dialogue we recommend be taught to students. The consistent use of the "Think Aloud" strategies by all school staff provides the basis for the success of this curriculum in decreasing undesirable behavior, while increasing the desired social skills. You will have better success changing the behavior of your students if all personnel are trained to use the common language in the "Think Aloud" strategies. This includes principals, secretarial staff, lunchroom and playground personnel, and auxiliary staff.

2. The posters reinforce the "Think Aloud" strategies. They follow each lesson and should be enlarged and displayed in the classrooms, hallways, and other areas of your school. Copy the student awards at the end of each section and present them to your students to reinforce the skills learned.

3. Each lesson has a story, activity, or discussion to "Establish the Need." Additional stories or activities under "Extended Activities" also will reinforce the skill in the lesson.

4. There is a sample letter to the parents should you choose to elicit parental support prior to beginning this curriculum.

5. This curriculum is based on the teaching methods of modeling the skill, providing opportunity for the students to role play, and reinforcing their skills with feedback. It is important that you actually model the desired skill using the "Think Aloud" strategies so your students can see the desired behavior.

6. The role play section of each lesson is meant to provide an opportunity for your students to practice the desired skill. This is the time to give feedback and correct any behavior. Research results are inconclusive as to whether role playing an incorrect example of each behavior is helpful for the students in learning the desired behavior. Some of the leaders in the field of social skill development believe that students learn the desired skill better if they are able to practice the contrast behavior; other feel this is unnecessary and a distraction. We have sometimes included a contrast role play under "Helpful Hints." You may use it at your discretion, knowing the needs of your students.

7. The most common reason for the failure of a social skills curriculum is in the lack of those skills generalizing to other environments. We correct this by providing "Transfer Training" activities to be done in other environments.

8. We hope you enjoy this curriculum, have fun with it, and use your own creativity to expand the lessons. We believe that for it to be the most effective, the skills should be taught in the order presented.

Suggestions for Teaching Social Skills

Now that you have the "why" and the ingredients, how do you start? Many schools start social skills curriculums, but they only last one to two years because staff lose interest, have other priorities, and don't see immediate impact.

Therefore, your school needs to know that a 4 to 5 year plan is essential. Start out slowly with classroom skills or friendship skills. Then proceed to other skills that are more difficult to master. Remember, all the staff, certified and non-certified, have to agree to do this. Set up meetings to define the needs of the school. Help each other to refine the program. Some skills will take longer to master than others. Listening, for example, is a life long skill that needs to be reinforced every year.

Each year you can set several skills as your targets and also review skills from previous years. Take a skill such as "Interrupting." Let's say you are going to teach the skill on Monday. Proceed through the whole lesson. Then, the rest of the week, review "Think Aloud" strategies. Do this review for two weeks and then as needed throughout the year. If problems arise, gently remind your students to repeat—either individually or in a group—the "think aloud" strategies. This skill will probably need to be reviewed. Plus, new students to the school are not aware of previous skills taught. Keep posters on the walls every year to remind your students of common language.

Another suggestion is to have the principal reinforce whatever skill you are working on when he or she does announcements. Leadership helps keep the skills moving and reinforces the positive aspects and results. You can also involve parents through parent/teacher conferences, PTA meetings, and newsletters. Community involvement is essential. Most parents want their children to have good social skills, but parents need help reinforcing them at home.

Some staff or schools are always changing curriculum—looking for the magic answer to solve all problems. Let's be realistic. Changing behavior and starting new programs *involves* hard work, determination, enthusiasm, and a concentrated effort over a long period of time. Schools with positive philosophies and a staff who work as a team to change negative behaviors always succeed because children and parents know what the expectations are.

There is no set way or philosophy to teaching social skills. Schools that stay with a social skills programs and: (1) are consistent and positive, (2) follow through with lessons, (3) involve parents; (4) define and refine programs through committee and staff meetings, (5) have all staff involved, (6) use common language, and (7) establish long term goals (4 to 5 years) will survive. The results will be positive benefits to the children. Both parents and teachers will be working together to improve the social skills of all children so they can learn in a positive environment.

Our Class is Studying Social Skills!

Dear Parent::

Our class is beginning a social skills curriculum. Your child will be learning better ways to resolve conflict, make friends and follow rules. These skills will help your children feel better about themselves, make decisions, handle stress and choose the best action in a given situation. Our belief is that in teaching children appropriate social skills, there is less need for correction of behavior.

We ask that you help reinforce these social skills at home. For each lesson there will be an activity to do at home. The purpose of these activities is to help your children do these skills in any environment.

There are seven areas of skills your children will learn with specific lessons under each area. The seven areas are:

1. Classroom Skills
2. Friendship Skills
3. Expressing Feelings
4. Relieving Stress
5. Solving Problems
6. Replacement Skills
7. Self Acceptance

Thank you for your support. Please call me if you have any concerns or questions.

Your Children's Teacher

Teacher's Screening Checklist

_____   _____   _____

Student's Name   Rated By   Date

Directions:

Circle the appropriate letter for each question. Rate this child in comparison with other children in the class.

Key:

5—Very often—means daily occurrence

3—Sometimes—means 2 to 3 times a week

1—Seldom—means 0 occurrence

I. Classroom Skills

1. Does the student listen to instructions or directions?   5   4   3   2   1
2. Does the student complete assignments on time?   5   4   3   2   1
3. Does the student follow classroom rules?   5   4   3   2   1
4. Does the student cooperate with a work partner?   5   4   3   2   1
5. Is the student prepared for class?   5   4   3   2   1

II. Interpersonal Relationships

1. Is the student accepted by most of his or her classmates?   5   4   3   2   1
2. Does the student have one or more friends?   5   4   3   2   1
3. Is the student often a victim of teasing?   5   4   3   2   1
4. Is the student respectful of other's property?   5   4   3   2   1
5. Is the student excluded by his or her peers?   5   4   3   2   1

III. Identifying and Expressing Feelings

1. Can the student express feelings in an appropriate way?   5   4   3   2   1
2. Does the student show understanding of other's feelings?   5   4   3   2   1
3. Does the student express unusual or extreme feelings?   5   4   3   2   1

IV. Relieving Stress

1. Can the student accept losing or failing?	5	4	3	2	1
2. Does the student handle changes in the daily routine?	5	4	3	2	1
3. Does the student over or under react to situations?	5	4	3	2	1
4. Does the student show signs of anxiety, nervousness, or stress?	5	4	3	2	1
5. Does the student defend his or her rights?	5	4	3	2	1

V. Problem Solving/Decision Making

1. Does the student accept responsibility for his or her actions?	5	4	3	2	1
2. Is the student able to make a decision independently?	5	4	3	2	1
3. Does the student overreact to minor problems?	5	4	3	2	1

VI. Replacement Skills

1. Does the student express anger appropriately?	5	4	3	2	1
2. Does the student avoid fights?	5	4	3	2	1
3. Does the student work out problems with friends by talking and compromising?	5	4	3	2	1
4. Does the student avoid situations which may cause problems?	5	4	3	2	1

VII. Self Acceptance

1. Does the student like himself or herself?	5	4	3	2	1
2. Does the student avoid putting down self and others?	5	4	3	2	1
3. Does the student tolerate differences in others?	5	4	3	2	1

Dennis Hanken, Ed.S. and Judith Kennedy, Ed.S.

Lesson 1: Being Prepared for Class

Objective: Students will have materials ready for class activities.

Materials Needed: Paper, pencil, rulers, crayons, scissors, books, reward item.

Establish the Need: Read the stories, "Remember Your Materials, Matt" and "Beth" on the next page. Lead a discussion on "Why is it important to be organized and prepared for class? What might happen if you don't have the right materials?"

Procedures:

Step 1: Model the skill:

A. Part of being organized is having materials ready for a class activity.

B. Demonstrate using "Think Aloud" strategies gathering the right materials:

> (1) What materials do I need? (2) Where do I look? (3) Gather materials; (4) Am I ready to start?

Helpful Hints: Read the stories (next page). Have your materials ready for presentation. Discuss which materials are appropriate for different subjects and which are not.

Step 2: Role play with feedback:

A. Ask your students to display their materials on their desks for math class.

B. Have your students gather correct materials for reading and give feedback to each other. Provide feedback throughout role playing.

Helpful Hints: Discuss how toys and other materials not needed create distractions to students. Ask each student to gather materials not needed (i.e., toys, rubber bands, etc.). Discuss why we don't want unneeded articles.

Step 3: Transfer training:

A. **School:** Inform the art, music, and computer teachers of the content of the lesson. Ask them to compliment a child who has the necessary materials for class.

B. **Home/Community:** You have to set the table. Plan where the plates and utensils are to be placed. Visualize what the table needs to look like. What utensils do you need? How many of each?

C. **Peers:** You are staying overnight at a friend's house. List the items you will need to pack.

Helpful Hints: Use items B and C as homework assignments and have their parents sign and return.

Comments: Rewards could be pencils, stickers, positive comments.

Extended Activities: Art projects: Paper clip structure, marshmallows/toothpick structure: anything requiring students to have their materials ready. Compile a survival list of things needed for a camping trip. "Classroom Skills Award," page 18.

"Remember Your Materials, Matt"

Matt, the mouse, went looking for food one day. Matt lived in the basement of a huge house. There was always plenty of food on the floor, especially in the TV room where all the adults ate while watching TV. There were only a couple of problems in that big house. There was Jumbo, the cat, and that wonderful machine called the vacuum cleaner. But, Matt knew how to get away from both of these as well as the adults. Matt's parents and older brothers and sisters who often played school told him to be prepared when he hunted for food. They told him to be sure to follow certain trails, wear his glasses (he was nearsighted and couldn't see things far away), to wear his helmet and mirror so he could see things behind him, and to not ever forget his tennis sneakers; otherwise he would slip and slide all over.

One of Matt's problems was that he didn't always think ahead and often would forget things. His family and friends always would remind him, but he never took them *seriously*. One day he was looking for food and the big cat came around the corner and started to chase him. Matt was running as hard as he could, but then he remembered he forgot his sneakers. He was slipping all over the place. Not only that, he couldn't see very well because he had forgotten his glasses, too. When he was about to give up, he saw an opening to the basement and he rushed in just in time to avoid the cat's paw.

Matt, the mouse, learned an important lesson that day. He learned that if others remind you to be prepared and you don't take them seriously, someday, when you don't bring the things you need, you could be surprised and *unprepared*. Then it will be too late to worry because you didn't listen and remember. Matt just pretended to be prepared and almost got caught by the cat. From then on, Matt, the mouse, was always prepared and ready for any surprises or traps.

"Beth"

Beth was invited to stay overnight at Amy's house. Her mother reminded her all day to pack the things she would need as she was being picked up at 4:00. At 3:45, her mother checked to see if Beth was packed. She had played outside and watched TV, but she had not packed! She hurried to her room and grabbed things and put them in her suitcase.

When she got to Amy's house, Beth discovered she had forgotten her pajamas, her toothbrush, and her asthma medication.

1. Why did Beth forget the things she needed?

2. What do you need to do to be prepared for something?

Lesson 1:   Being Prepared for Class

1. What materials do I need?

2. Where do I look?

3. Gather materials.

4. Am I ready to start?

CLASSROOM SKILLS

Classroom Skills Award

to

_____

for mastering the skill of

_____

Date _____

Teacher signature _____

Lesson 2: Listening

Objective: Students will sit quietly and look at the teacher.

Materials Needed: Puppets and story ("Peter Cottontail" or "Three Little Pigs"), or the story on the next page.

Establish the Need: Stories: "Three Little Pigs" or "Peter Cottontail," also "Nobody's Listening," (see the next page). Discuss the consequences for not listening.

Procedures:

Step 1: Model the skill:

A. Look at your students around the room to see if they are listening.

B. Demonstrate listening using "Think Aloud" strategies:

(1) Look. (2) Stay still. (3) Think.

Helpful Hints: "Look" means to look at the person talking. "Stay still" means seat to seat, back to back, feet to floor. "Think" means thinking about what is said. Have your students repeat back to ensure understanding.

Step 2: Role play with feedback:

A. Divide in groups of three. One student talks (see helpful hints), one listens, and one gives feedback.

B. Give 3 to 5 part directions by row or pods. Have your students help to evaluate.

Helpful Hints: (1) Use a favorite TV show, food, vacation, activity, and so forth. Grade 1, use 3-part directions; grades 2 to 3 use 4- to 5-part directions. Have all of the students in the group talk at the same time for contrast. Discuss the results.

Step 3: Transfer training:

A. **School:** Ask the music teacher to give your students a new song to learn and give feedback.

B. **Home/Community:** Have your students go home and listen to a discussion at the dinner table and see if it makes sense. Report back.

C. **Peers:** Discuss your last conversation with your best friend.

Helpful Hints: Verbal cues are helpful for students. Suggestions: "Is your body ready to listen?" "Listening ears." "Are you looking at the teacher?"

Comments: Listening is a vital skill for survival in school. Children who are poor listeners usually make less progress than their peers. Children usually do not know the steps to good listening-they need to be taught this in school.

Extended Activities: (1) "Nobody's Listening," (puppets, story) see the next page, (2) "I Spy" game, (3) Reporter (see the next page). Books: Lionni, Leo. *Frederick,* New York: Knopf, 1990. Wiseman Bernard, *Morris and Boris.* New York: Putnam Publishing Group.

"Nobody's Listening"

Materials Needed: 3 puppets

Instructions: Introduce the three puppets and tell the name of the story.

Mike:	Hey, I'm glad everyone is here! We need to plan our camping trip.
Sam:	Speaking of camping, my uncle went camping in Yellowstone and they saw three bears and they were....
Seth:	Three bears! That's nothing. When my cousin went to Glacier they saw four bears and a moose!
Sam:	You interrupted me! You weren't listening!
Mike:	Neither of you is listening. I was trying to talk to you about planning our camping trip.
Sam:	He's right. We weren't listening. We can't plan our trip unless we listen to each other.
Mike:	I think we all need to follow the three steps of listening.
Seth:	What do you mean?
Mike:	First, we have to look at the person who is talking. Second, we have to stay still. Third, we have to think about what the person is saying.
Sam:	How do we think about what the person is saying?
Mike:	Well, I try to repeat what the person said. That way I know I was listening.
Seth:	Good idea! Let's listen to each other and plan our camping trip.

Questions for your students:

1. What did the boys need to do?
2. What are the steps of listening?

"The Reporter"

Ask the children to choose an article-a recent drawing or other project, an article of clothing, some other personal item-they'd like to tell the group about. Then have them sit in a circle. Explain that they'll be playing a game to practice listening skills. Ask one student to be the first "Reporter."

Explain the game: The "Reporter" pretends to interview another student about the object that student is holding or has selected and asks, "Please tell us about that?" The person being interviewed tells the reporter two things about the object. The reporter repeats the two things said. The person being interviewed then becomes the "Reporter" and interviews someone else.

Have the reporter begin. Continue around the circle until every student has had a chance to be the reporter and to be interviewed.

Lesson 2: Listening

1. Look.

2. Stay still.

3. Think.

CLASSROOM SKILLS

Lesson 3: Following Verbal Directions

Objective: Students will follow verbal directions given by a teacher or other staff person.

Materials Needed: 3 x 5 card with a list of instructions (i.e., go to the chalkboard, pick up the chalk, write the date, set the chalk down, go back to your desk); Look, Stay Still, Think-reminder to listen.

Establish the Need: Erin was thinking about the swimming party she was invited to. She didn't even hear the teacher give the directions for the art project. The teacher said, "Now go get the materials in the order I said." Erin had no idea what to do. She sat and looked around her. (1) Why did Erin not know what to do? (2) Have you ever missed hearing directions? Read the story "Deer Safety" on the next page.

Procedures:

Step 1: Model the skill:

A. Have your students read the instructions on a 3 x 5 card to you.

B. Use "Think Aloud" strategies to narrate as you do the instructions.

(1) Repeat the instructions; (2) Ask any questions; (3) Do instructions.

C. Discuss modeling and have your students evaluate if you followed directions.

Helpful Hints: For novelty, leave out an instruction and have your students identify what is left out.

Step 2: Role play with feedback:

A. Pair your students. Have one student give other student a 2-step direction. Evaluate following the direction.

B. Move to a 3- to 4-step direction. Emphasize how important listening is as the amount of information increases.

Helpful Hints: Make up a 2-step direction. Teach: listen for "key" words. Have two students demonstrate not following directions for contrast. Children with ADD or auditory problems may have trouble doing this.

Step 3: Transfer training:

A. **School:** In PE, explain a new game and give verbal praise for following directions.

B. **Home/Community:** Parents assign their children a 2- to 4-step direction depending upon their grade levels (grade 1, 2 steps; grades 2 to 3, 3- and 4-steps).

C. **Peers:** Learn the directions for various games like "Redrover" or "Twister," and take turns explaining and listening.

Comments: You could use buttons with "I am a good listener" on them.

Extended Activities: Send a child on an errand outside of class (2- to 4-step direction); play "Simon Says," game, "Twister" game, or "Treasure Hunt" game (walk to bookshelf and look on bottom shelf under big book); give verbal directions to a fun activity; put verbal directions in the format of a "map."

"Deer Safety"

One day deep in the forest two yearling deer (fawns) were listening to their mother (doe). She was talking to them about deer season and also about cars on the highways, two very important parts to deer survival. The names of the deer were Mona and Whino. The problem with these two deer was that they had difficulty listening to directions because they were so busy complaining and "bugging" each other. Mother deer told them over and over again what to do, but they thought "no problem." Well, the first day of deer season came, and the two were bouncing around the forest, carefree as ever. All of a sudden, a shot was heard and Mona felt a sting in her left ear. Whino took off like a scared Jackrabbit and ran straight in front of a car. Splat!!! Whino wobbles to her feet. She moved a little slow, but managed to catch up to Mona. They finally made it back to mom with some stories to tell. Mom listened and said, "I think I told you about this several times." Well, you can believe next deer season was really different because they listened to mom more intently and followed every verbal direction. By the way, Mom changed their names from Mona and Whino to Zig and Zag.

Lesson 3: Following Verbal Directions

1. Repeat instructions.

2. Ask any questions.

3. Do instructions.

CLASSROOM SKILLS

Lesson 4: Following Written Directions

Objective: Students will be able to read written directions and follow them without teacher assistance.

Materials Needed: Chalkboard, worksheets.

Establish the Need: Discuss written rules in school and class. Why is it important to read and follow, i.e., bathroom signs, street signs, danger signs, wet floor, and so forth? Discuss.

Procedures:

Step 1: Model the skill:

A. Write some directions on the chalkboard.

B. Model reading and carrying out directions using "Think Aloud" strategies.

(1) Read all directions. (2) Think about them. (3) Do it. (4) Check your work.

C. Students will identify the steps they observed.

Helpful Hints: Your directions might include: go to your desk, pick up a red pen, go to the last desk in row 5, lay the red pen down.

Step 2: Role play with feedback:

A. Your students read the directions and complete a worksheet.

B. Have your students follow the steps for addressing an envelope. Give feedback.

Helpful Hints: Draw a rectangle containing 6 boxes, for an additional activity.

Worksheet Directions:

1. In box #1, put an 0.

2. In box #2, draw a square.

3. In box #3, draw a smiley face.

4. In box #4, print your name

5. In box #5, print a 3.

6. In box #6, draw a tree.

Step 3: Transfer training:

A. **School:** Write directions for an activity on the board instead of giving them verbally.

B. **Home/Community:** Have the parents give their children a simple recipe to follow, i.e., no-bake cookies.

C. **Peers:** A friend writes you directions to find his or her house.

Comments: Tasks will need to be simple enough to avoid frustrations.

Extended Activities: Read the directions for a board game in small groups and play the game. Your class offers many opportunities to check for and reinforce following written directions. Have your students bring something they bought at a store and read the directions to the class, i.e., assembling a toy, combination lock, game. "Classroom Skills Award," page 18.

Lesson 4:   Following Written Directions

1. Read all directions.

2. Think about them.

3. Do it.

4. Check work.

CLASSROOM SKILLS

Dennis Hanken, Ed.S. and Judith Kennedy, Ed.S.

Lesson 5: Ignoring Distractions/ Staying on Task

Objective: Students will learn to remain on task despite hall, playground, and classroom distractions.

Materials Needed: Chalkboard, academic worksheets.

Establish the Need: Using puppets, show a puppet staying on task with another puppet doing a distracting behavior. Discuss what should you do if the child next to you is very distracting while you are trying to work?

Procedures:

Step 1: Model the skill:

A. Tell your students the steps to stay on task.

B. Portray a student staying on task using "Think Aloud" strategies:

(1) Listen. (2) Gather materials. (3) Begin. (4) Work quietly. (5) Ignore distractions. (6) Stay on task. (Define ignore: keep working in spite of what others are doing.)

Step 2: Role play with feedback:

A. Give your students worksheets and tell them you will be evaluating how well they stay on task. Provide feedback.

B. Review the rules and do another activity with worksheets. Evaluate their performance.

Helpful Hints: For contrast, create a noise while your students are working or have them attempt to distract one another. Incidences where students were distracted need to be handled in a non-judgmental manner. Discuss how hard it is to work in confusion.

Step 3: Transfer training:

A. **School:** Have the music teacher note when your students remain on task by giving positive comments to them.

B. **Home/Community:** Inform the parents of skills their students are learning. Ask them to reinforce on-task behavior during chores or homework.

C. **Peers:** Have your students evaluate how well they do when a classmate tries to distract them.

Comments: Your students will have vastly different abilities to remain on task and ignore distractions. Consider other interventions for those students who seem truly unable to stay on task.

Extended Activities: Have your students give themselves a point for each time they stay on task during an activity. The classroom offers many opportunities to reinforce students who stay on task despite distractions. There are very good interventions in *The Attention Deficit Disorders Intervention Manual* by S.B. McCarney.

Lesson 5: Staying on Task

1. Listen.

2. Gather materials.

3. Begin.

4. Work quietly.

5. Ignore distractions.

6. Stay on task.

CLASSROOM SKILLS

Lesson 6: Finishing Assignments

Objective: Students will complete the majority of their assignments within a reasonable time.

Materials Needed: Chalkboard, kitchen timer.

Establish the Need: Discuss what happens if the teacher doesn't finish the report cards, or the principal writes half of your name on a reward, or you only get half of a lunch. Read the story on the next page.

Procedures:

Step 1: Model the skill:

A. Put several math problems on the board.

B. Demonstrate using "Think Aloud" strategies.

> (1) What do I need to do? (2) Get materials. (3) Get started. (4) Keep working. (5) Finish.

C. Set the timer for two minutes and then model the skill.

D. Have your students repeat the "Think Aloud" strategies.

Helpful Hints: Discuss the importance of having the needed materials.

Step 2: Role play with feedback:

A. Give your students math worksheets at mastery level. Have them role play how to complete a task on time. Set the timer.

B. When the timer goes off, ask your students how they followed procedures. Give praise and stickers.

Helpful Hints: Use stickers for completing work on time. For contrast have your students waste time and not finish. Discuss their feelings. Give feedback.

Step 3: Transfer training:

A. **School:** Use this as a class project for a popcorn party. Every completed assignment is a point. Count up the points on Friday.

B. **Home/Community:** Have the parents set up a job at home with time limits and use the homework page to report back.

C. **Peers:** Have your students set up a craft project at home and use steps 1 through 5 in completing the project.

Helpful Hints: This will also reinforce goal setting.

Comments: Discuss the consequences for not completing their work. (1) Failure, (2) punishment, (3) low grades, (4) adult rejection or anger.

Extended Activities: Class project for group party. Competitive game-divide your class into half, one group does more completed assignments and receives an award or whatever the group decides. Read the story on the next page. See *The Attention Deficit Disorders Intervention Manual* by S.B. McCarney for more interventions, pages 9-11. "Classroom Skills Award," page 18 and "Homework Gram," page 32.

Dusty, the Dawdler

Dusty was poky in everything he did. His parents had to tell him 3 or 4 times to put his toys away, get ready to go, or get ready for bed. He had the same problem in school. He would "dawdle" and not finish his math work or his spelling lists. Everyone was always telling Dusty to hurry up and finish. He even had trouble finishing a meal.

One day Dusty's mom told him they would go swimming as soon as he finished picking up his room and putting things away. Dusty loved swimming and excitedly began picking up his clothes and toys and putting them away. But, as he was picking up his train, he decided to see if it would still go through the tunnel. He played and played with it, not noticing how much time had passed. Finally his mom came to his room to see if he was ready to go swimming. Dusty still hadn't picked up most of his things. His mom said he still needed to clean his room, and that it was too late to go swimming. Dusty was disappointed.

Questions for your students:

1. Why did Dusty miss out on swimming?
2. What should Dusty do in the future to avoid missing out on fun activities? (Hint: Keep working on a project until it is done.)

Lesson 6:   Finishing Assignments

1. What do I need to do?

2. Get materials.

3. Get started.

4. Keep working.

5. Finish.

CLASSROOM SKILLS

Homework Gram

Student _____

Date _____

Skill: _____

"Think Aloud" strategies used: _____

_____

_____

With whom will I use this skill? _____

_____

When? _____

What was the result? _____

_____

How did I do?_____

_____

Lesson 7:   Asking for Assistance or Information

Objective: To teach students to ask for help appropriately and to wait quietly until they get assistance or their question answered.

Materials Needed: Story "Ask and You Will Receive" and "Don't Panic" on the following page.

Establish the Need: Have your students all raise their hands and call for help. Discuss how no one can get helped if all are "clamoring" for help.

Procedures:

Step 1: Model the skill:

A. Use "Think Aloud" strategies to model asking for help or asking questions:

> (1) Try to do the task myself. (2) Decide if help is needed. (3) Raise my hand. (4) Sit quietly and wait. (5) Say "thank you" when done.

Step 2: Role play with feedback:

A. Have your students individually ask for help using "Think Aloud" strategies.

B. Evaluate and provide feedback.

Helpful Hints: It is important that children see how disruptive everyone asking at once can be. If you have a student who has a particular difficulty with this, you might try the interventions on the following pages. Have several students calling out for help, and coming to the teacher and demonstrating inappropriate asking. Discuss the results.

Step 3: Transfer training:

A. **School:** Ask your lunchroom staff to reinforce your students who ask for help appropriately.

B. **Home/Community:** You can't find your swimsuit and you ask your mom to help.

C. **Peers:** You ask a friend to teach you the rules of a game.

Comments: Children who are impulsive will have more difficulty with this skill. It will help them if you have a system in your classroom that minimizes waiting, such as peer assistance.

Extended Activities: (1) Ask your brother, mom, dad, or sister to help you fly a kite, tie your shoe, or find your coat. (2) Tell the playground staff your class is practicing "Asking for Help." Ask them to reinforce appropriate asking. There are more interventions in *The Attention Deficit Disorders Intervention Manual* by S.B. McCarney on pages 14-17 and 20-23.

Ask and You Shall Receive

One day Judy (mother of four ducklings) was taking her foursome on a long hike to find a new pond for bathing and food. The ducklings could care less and Judy was getting very impatient at their lack of cooperation. She said to them, "You can't listen to me if you all talk at once and you are giving me a duckache (headache)." Judy decided just to sit and wait for them to become appropriate. Finally the older duckling (by three minutes) said, "Could we all hold feathers and I will lead behind you? We are getting better at following you in a straight line." (Good idea!) One little duckling waved his foot and said, "We can do this if we all cooperate." All the rest sat quietly and waited. Mother said, "I like it when you ask for help or assistance in a nice manner. "Thank you," said the ducklings and they found the pond within a minute with everyone's cooperation.

Don't Panic

One day Kim (a lovely little chipmunk) got lost. She couldn't find her home (a log), and she couldn't find her friends. She was definitely in a panic situation. She even started to cry, "What am I going to do?" Well, along came Bob (skunk) and says to Kim, "Why are you crying little chipmunk?" but Kim was so anxious she could hardly speak. So Bob just tried to talk about different things, her age, her friends, etc. Finally, Kim said, "Do you know my mother Hilda Chipmunk? We live near the vacant mine near two trees that split from one huge tree?" "Of course I do," said Bob. "Will you help me find my way home?," asked Kim. "Yes, of course," answered Bob. "Thank you," Kim said, "I feel better already." Bob helped Kim find her way home.

Lesson 7:   Asking for Assistance or Information

1. Try to do task myself.

2. Decide help is needed.

3. Raise my hand.

4. Sit quietly and wait.

5. Say *"thank you"* when done.

CLASSROOM SKILLS

Lesson 8:   Saying *Please* and *Thank You*

Objective: Students will say "please" prior to making a request and "thank you" after their request is answered.

Materials Needed: Puppets.

Establish the Need: Children with good manners are well liked by adults and peers. Using puppets, show one using "please" and "thank you" and another one responding. Discuss: What do we say when we want something from someone? What do we say when we get it? When you say "please" and "thank you," is that an act of kindness?

Procedures:

Step 1: Model the skill:

Use two hand puppets to model saying "please" and "thank you," using "Think Aloud" strategies.

(1) Think: What do I say when I want something? "Please"

(2) Think: What do I say when someone says or does something nice for me? "Thank you."

Step 2: Role play with feedback:

A. Role play having your students asking for things from you. Using "please" and "thank you."

B. In pairs have your students ask each other for a pencil using "please" and "thank you."

Helpful Hints: Shy students may want to use puppets. For contrast have your students ask in an inappropriate method, (give me that, not using "thank you").

Step 3: Transfer training:

A. **School:** Have your students ask for things throughout the week from the principal, secretary, and other teachers.

B. **Home/Community:** Ask your students to go home and ask for something using "please" and "thank you." How do your parents feel about how you asked?

C. **Peers:** Ask a friend to play with you during recess or on weekends. Compare the results when you do use "please" and "thank you" and when you don't use these words.

Helpful Hints: Shy students need to ask someone with whom they are comfortable.

Comments: Sometimes having a thank you card for those who can't verbally say it might be helpful at first. This skill may have been taught at home, but it applies at school and can be generalized at school. Have your students decide who has given a gift to school and how to thank them. Model using "please" and "thank you." "Classroom Skills Award," page 18 and "Homework Gram," page 32.

Lesson 8: Saying *Please* and *Thank You*

1. Think: What do I say when I want something?

   Please

2. Think: What do I say when someone says or does something nice for me?

   Thank you

CLASSROOM SKILLS

Lesson 9: Participating in Discussions

Objective: To teach students to say something during class discussion using the right voice and staying on topic.

Materials Needed: Story "Yaz, The Daydreamer" and "Talk About Staying On Subject" on the following page.

Establish the Need: Have three students come up front, whisper to each individual children a topic they will discuss (a different topic for each). Have all three students discuss their topic at the same time. Discuss with your class how confusing it is when people talk at the same time and do not stay on a single topic.

Procedures:

Step 1: Model the skill:

Model with one student how to have a discussion and stay on the same subject using "Think Aloud" strategies:

(1) Look at the person who is talking. (2) Raise your hand and wait quietly. (3) Stay on the subject. (4) Use the right voice.

Step 2: Role play with feedback:

Have your students discuss a timely subject using "Think Aloud" strategies. Evaluate.

Helpful Hints: Timely subjects could include current news, the season of the year, pets, or a favorite activity, movie, or TV show. Instruct three students to add irrelevant, interrupting talk to a classroom discussion. Evaluate.

Step 3: Transfer training:

A. **School:** Ask the Speech Therapist to come in as a guest to lead a class discussion. Reinforce the students who participate appropriately.

B. **Home/Community:** Tell your family about your social skill lesson during dinner.

C. **Peers:** Discuss something with a group of friends. Report back.

Comments: You may need to encourage shy students to add something to the discussion. Learning good classroom discussion skills will help your students participate in conversations in other settings. Use smaller groups or one-to-one first.

Extended Activities: (1) Set aside a period for class discussion and reinforce correct techniques. (2) Divide your class into small groups with a leader and a topic to discuss. "Classroom Skills Award," page 18 and "Homework Gram," page 32.

Yaz, The Daydreamer

Deep in the heart of the school year, Yaz was doing his usual daydreaming about the weekend when all of a sudden he heard his name. He looked up with a blank look in his eyes. Say what? The teacher was asking him about the discussion of a story they had just read. The teacher suspected Yaz was daydreaming, but she also felt that Yaz would like the story. Yaz tended to fade out during classroom discussion because he had a short attention span.

"Well, enough is enough," said Yaz. "I hate being called on when I am daydreaming." He decided right then that from now on he would listen more, look at the teacher when she is talking, and raise his hand to talk. "I can live with this and besides the teacher always knows when I am daydreaming. In the long run, I will be much happier with this plan."

Talk About Staying on the Subject

One early fall day during a group discussion, the teacher asked Judy if she could tell the class about her summer. She said, "I would be glad to." But during her summary, she started talking about her family, friends, and dog. The teacher said, "I just wanted a short talk about your summer, Judy. What did you do?" Judy said, "I didn't stay on the subject of summer. I started talking about all kinds of things." After this talk with Judy, other students did a better job staying on the subject-summer!!

Lesson 9:   Participating In Discussions

1. Look at the person who is talking.

2. Raise your hand and wait quietly.

3. Stay on the subject.

4. Use the right voice.

CLASSROOM SKILLS

Lesson 10: Working Effectively with a Partner

Objective: Students will work cooperatively with a partner during class activities.

Materials Needed: Drawing paper, markers or chalkboard to write the rules.

Establish the Need: Help your students to see that each of them is affected if the project is not done. Some classrooms are set up in pods of two to four students. Does this help prepare students for projects or activities?

Ask your students what would happen if only a few construction workers showed up to build a building.

Procedures:

Step 1: Model the skill:

A. Model with a student working effectively using "Think Aloud" strategies:

> (1) Share materials. (2) Decide who does what. (3) Share my ideas. (4) Listen to my partner's ideas. (5) Work until finished.

B. Discuss with your students the skill components and the modeling.

Helpful Hints: Suggested activity: make a poster together where your students have to share materials.

Step 2: Role play with feedback:

A. Assign your students in pairs and give them the task of drawing a picture of an animal they both agree on. Give feedback.

B. At the end of 10 to 15 minutes, elicit feedback from the partners who had difficulty. Give feedback.

C. Elicit a discussion from the partners where the project went smoothly. Provide feedback.

Helpful Hints: Give one piece of drawing paper and one half set of markers to each partner team. Allow 10 to 15 minutes for the task.

Step 3: Transfer training:

A. **School:** Ask the PE teacher to assign your students in pairs to use one set of equipment.

B. **Home/Community:** Assign your students the homework of setting the dinner table with someone else.

C. **Peers:** Assign your students in pairs and have them check out one set of equipment to use at recess. Elicit responses after recess. This could include one ball, jump rope, frisbee, kite.

Helpful Hints: You could use one basketball with each set of students. Give credit for how many baskets each made.

Comments: Working cooperatively is necessary for all relationships and should be taught until mastery is shown.

Extended Activities: Assign your students in pairs to solve puzzles, fill in crosswords, or make papier-mache items. This skill can be reinforced daily in cooperative learning groups. "Classroom Skills Award," page 18.

Lesson 10: Working Effectively with a Partner

1. Share materials.

2. Decide who does what.

3. Share my ideas.

4. Listen to partner's ideas.

5. Work until finished.

CLASSROOM SKILLS

Dennis Hanken, Ed.S. and Judith Kennedy, Ed.S.

Lesson 11: Finishing Our Work, Finding Something to Do

Objective: To have students self-check to be sure all items are completed on the task and to think of activities to do and choose one.

Materials Needed: Math worksheets, kitchen timer, items of interest (centers for students to choose from). Read the story, "The Right Decision," on the following page.

Establish the Need: "Have you ever gotten into trouble for being noisy, fooling around, or doing nothing when your teacher gave you some free time in class?" "What do you think your teacher thinks when you sit and do nothing?" "How do you feel when you've got nothing to do?"

Procedures:

Step 1: Model the skill:

A. Put a number of math problems on the board and tell your students you are going to model finishing your work.

B. Set a timer and use "Think Aloud" strategies:

   (1) Am I done? (2) Check my work. (3) What are my choices for free time? (4) Make the best choice.

C. With your students' input, write on the chalkboard a list of quiet activities to do when class is done with work.

D. Choose an activity.

Step 2: Role play with feedback:

A. Give your students math worksheets to be completed in 5 to 10 minutes. Set the timer. Have your students choose one activity to do when they have completed the work. At the end of time, elicit from your students feedback on problem areas.

B. Have your students complete work and pursue constructive free time without disrupting the class.

Helpful Hints: Give feedback throughout the work time. For contrast have your students complete their work and then disrupt the class. Give feedback.

Step 3: Transfer training:

A. **School:** Complete the assignments given by the computer teacher and choose a new activity.

B. **Home/Community:** Complete a household chore and decide on the first activity to do afterward.

C. **Peers:** Complete a project you are working on with a friend. It could be the activity from Lesson 10. Find a fun activity to do afterward.

Comments: It will be helpful for your students to learn the Premack Principle: "Work now, play later," for general life application. This skill also helps those students who have trouble planning free time activities.

Extended Activities: Have learning centers in your room from which your students may choose when their seat work is completed. Reward individual students in their progress of completing their seat work. "Classroom Skills Award," page 18 and "Homework Gram," page 32.

The Right Decision

One day Bubba finished his work and stared around the room. "My, my, now what am I going to do? Well, lets see, I could "bug" Mary and Joe. I could go to the bathroom and waste some time. I could pretend to clean out my desk. Oh! Oh!, the teacher is giving me one of those looks. We all get bored or have some free time now and then. I think I need to make good choices. I got it, I will go ask the teacher if I can help her or someone in the class. Gee, that decision makes me feel good and I won't get in trouble. I'll tell my parents and they will feel good about me too. Wow, isn't life a treat!!!"

Making the Right Choice

John & Mary were always the first two students done in Mr. Quick's room. But that's about all they had in common. John would finish his work and "bug" others and get into trouble. Mary, however, always found something to do-read a book, do some of her homework, or help others with their work. Mr. Quick decided to have a talk with John about his behavior. He said, "John, you have to decide which is best for you; me giving you negative attention or you finding something to do." John thought about this for several days. Then one day he talked to Mr. Quick. They worked out several things that John could do after he finished his work. John could now plan to do more things after school instead of serving detention or staying after school. John was not a "bad" boy, he just needed some ideas and choices.

Lesson 11: Finishing Your Work
Finding Something to Do

1. Am I done?

2. Check my work.

3. What are my choices for free time?

4. Make the best choice.

CLASSROOM SKILLS

Lesson 12: Interrupting

Objective: The student will learn how to interrupt the teacher when it is necessary.

Materials Needed: None.

Establish the Need: Read the stories, "Interrupting Ike" and "Feeling Ill," on the following page. Discuss.

Procedures:

Step 1: Model the skill:

Have two students talk and you demonstrate how to interrupt using "Think Aloud" strategies:

(1) Do I need to? (2) Raise my hand. (3) Wait or say, "Excuse me."

Helpful Hints: The first Step is most critical.

Step 2: Role play with feedback:

A. In 3s , have your students talk in pairs and then practice interrupting one at a time.

B. Interrupt two adults in front of children and have your students do the same.

Helpful Hints: This should be practiced on an on-going basis. This skill often takes longer to master than a 9-month time period. This is a life skill that needs reminders. Role play interrupting without using the four Steps and get a negative response or have a pair ignore the person who is interrupting.

Step 3: Transfer training:

A. **School:** A teacher and an adult are talking, and you need help with your work.

B. **Home/Community:** A parent is talking on the phone and you need to ask permission to go somewhere. Report back.

C. **Peers:** Your two best friends are talking secretively, but you need to ask one if you can borrow a book.

Helpful Hints: Most of the time students should wait until adults are done talking. If it is an emergency, interrupting is okay. Help your students to distinguish.

Comments: There is a risk in interrupting two or more people. You could receive a negative response or it could be "no big deal." Sometimes waiting is the best solution.

Extended Activities: Make a list of situations under the headings of: Not to Interrupt, Okay To Interrupt, Emergency. "Classroom Skills Award," page 18, and "Homework Gram," page 32.

Interrupting Ike

Ike was a boy in second grade. He hated to wait his turn. Every time he needed help, he would yell out, "Teacher, teacher, I need help!" It was very noisy for the other students when Ike would yell out. Sometimes the teacher would be helping someone else when Ike wanted help.

One day the teacher was helping Ike when all the other students in the class yelled, "Teacher, teacher, I need your help!!" "Ike's teacher said kindly to Ike; "Isn't it distracting when people yell out for help and don't wait or say, "excuse me." Ike realized that he had not been using the "Think Aloud" strategies for interrupting. He decided he would do the strategies each time he felt he needed help from now on.

Feeling Ill

John, a first grader, was always "bugging" people or interrupting adults and his classmates without using the proper strategies. One day John didn't feel very well and had to go to the bathroom immediately. However, his teacher and the principal were talking and he didn't know what to do. Finally he just said, "Excuse me, I have to go to the bathroom." His teacher said, "Thank you for your good manners. Yes, go right away." She knew something was wrong with John. After he got back to class, John said to himself, "It is a lot easier to be polite and ask in a nice voice than it is to interrupt or 'bug' others."

Lesson 12: Interrupting

1. Do I need to?

2. Raise my hand.

3. Wait or say...
"Excuse me."

CLASSROOM SKILLS

Dennis Hanken, Ed.S. and Judith Kennedy, Ed.S.

Lesson 13: Trying When it is Hard

Objective: Students will learn to persevere and try different ways when getting frustrated.

Materials Needed: Chalkboard, worksheets of scrambled words that are fairly difficult, stories, "Keep Trying" and "Don't Give Up, If You Want To Succeed," on the following page.

Establish the Need: Discuss the feeling of frustration and that all people feel frustrated sometimes. Discuss how good a person feels when he or she tries to do something hard and succeeds. Read the stories on the next page and discuss.

Procedures:

Step 1: Model the skill:

Model on the chalkboard doing a hard math problem using "Think Aloud" strategies:

> (1) Start work. (2) Consider options: (a) complete the task the best I can, (b) ask for help, (c) try another way, (d) come back to it later.

Step 2: Role play with feedback:

A. Have your students attempt difficult worksheets with scrambled words for 3 to 5 minutes. Stop your students and discuss their feelings.

B. Discuss other ways your students could attempt a task, i.e., partners, cooperative groups.

C. More role play using appropriate choices of trying when it is hard.

Helpful Hints: We are trying to get students to attempt new and difficult tasks, but also to find other ways to go about a task that is too hard. Have your students role play crying or giving up when they can't solve problems. Discuss.

Step 3: Transfer training:

A. **School:** Ask the PE teacher to have your students attempt a task that will be quite challenging and to explore other ways to do the task.

B. **Home/Community:** Ask parents to assign household chores that their children find difficult to do.

C. **Peers:** Do an activity with a friend that you think you can't do, i.e., roller-skate, cartwheel, ride a two-wheel bike, ice skate, and so forth.

Helpful Hints: Reward your students for attempting difficult tasks. (Sticker, etc.).

Comments: This is particularly good for children who fear failure. Be sure to encourage these children to try new things, but be careful not to ask too much of them.

Extended Activities: (1) There are many skills which will be taught in the classroom where you will want to reinforce trying when it is hard (new math concepts, reading tasks, scissor skills, tying shoes, memorizing). (2) Read "The Little Engine That Could." Discuss feeling in the story and what might happen if the engine had not tried. "Classroom Skills Award," page 18, and "Homework Gram," page 32.

Keep Trying

It was a foggy day in River City and Alex walked to school for another shot at educational progress. He was in a kind of sluggish mood. It didn't matter to him whether he went to school or took a fantasy trip to Disney World in his mind.

Anyway, about 10:15, Ms. Difficult, the math teacher, gave the whole class a very difficult assignment. "Thanks a lot," he said to himself! The more he did on this worksheet the harder it got. Alex decided to ask the teacher for help. He did and felt okay about it, but he couldn't ask her on every problem. So he skipped the ones he couldn't do and then decided he needed a break. Well, I guess I'll go to the bathroom. He came back and took a couple of deep breaths and finished the assignment. He thought to himself, getting uptight and worrying about it doesn't get it done. Sometimes asking for help, taking a break, and coming back to it later helps. You think with less clutter in your mind. If you just stick with your problem, and try when it is hard, it's truly amazing what you can accomplish.

Don't Give Up, If You Want to Succeed!

Jody was a first grade student who every time she found something too hard would just say, "What's the use" and give up!! After several months of this, her teacher, Ms. Understanding, and her parents were very frustrated with her behavior. They decided on a plan. Instead of giving up, Jody would (1) start to work (2) complete the work the best she could, (3) ask for help or come back to it later. She could also ask for help from her parents. Her parents would check her work. It seemed everyone was working to help solve the problem. Jody felt she was doing better and knowing that everyone cared about what she did helped her work even harder. She seemed to like getting attention for positive reasons rather than negative ones.

Lesson 13: Trying When It's Hard

1. Start work.

2. Consider options:

a. Complete the task the best I can.

b. Ask for help.

c. Try another way.

d. Come back to it later.

CLASSROOM SKILLS

Lesson 14: Introducing Yourself to Peers and Adults

Objective: Students will introduce themselves to peers and adults.

Materials Needed: Story on the following page.

Establish the Need: Discuss with your students the feelings of fear in meeting new people. Discuss appropriate times and places to introduce yourself.

Read and discuss the story, "Dear Ms. Flanders," on the next page.

Procedures:

Step 1: Model the skill:

A. With another student, simulate a social situation; then introduce yourself.

B. Use "Think Aloud" strategies:

(1) Do I want to meet the person? (2) Is this a good time? (3) How do I approach him or her? (4) Introduce myself.

Helpful Hints: Be sure to model greeting the other person, saying your name, asking that person's name, and starting a conversation.

Step 2: Role play with feedback:

A. Pair your students and have them practice introducing themselves.

B. Rotate through the groups and offer feedback and correction.

Helpful Hints: Have your students introduced inappropriately and give feedback.

Step 3: Transfer training:

A. **School:** Introduce yourself to a student you do not know on the playground.

B. **Home/Community:** Introduce yourself to a friend of your parents.

C. **Peers:** Introduce yourself to a new child and report back to your class.

Comments: This is a skill that is difficult even for adults and should be practiced whenever possible.

Extended Activities: (1) Have your students self-report on making introduction. (2) Have your students introduce themselves to visitors to the class (3) Have a class party with your students inviting a relative. Each student introduces himself or herself to one guest. (4) During Grandparent's Day, have your children introduce themselves. "Friendship Award," page 55 and "Homework Gram," page 32.

Dear Ms. Flanders

Dear Ms. Flanders:

"I have moved to a different school. What can I do not to be scared and shy?"

_____

Dear Student:

Moving to a new school can be scary, but it can be exciting too! You could have a neat teacher, or find a friend who likes all the same things you do. Maybe you'll be the best basketball player or wear the coolest clothes.

It's normal to feel shy around people you don't know. So the solution to your problem is... get to know them! Don't wait for them to come to meet you, introduce yourself to them! It's not as scary as it sounds. All you do is decide if you want to meet someone and if now looks like it is a good time, then walk up to them, say your name and invite them to play with you. Let the kids at your new school see that you're friendly. Smile. Talk. Share your feelings. Treat your new friends the way you'd like to be treated. And don't feel you have to pick a best friend right away. Take your time! It's going to be a super year.

Ms. Flanders

1. What is the best thing to do when you feel shy around people you don't know?
2. What is the best way to treat your friends?

Lesson 14: Introducing Yourself to Peers and Adults

1. Do I want to meet the person?

2. Is this a good time?

3. How do I approach them?

4. Introduce myself.

FRIENDSHIP SKILLS

Friendship Award

to

_____

for using the skill of

_____

Date _____

_____

Lesson 15: Recognizing Other's Facial Expressions

Objective: The student will have a basic understanding of facial expressions, gestures and body language.

Materials Needed: Pictures from magazines depicting different feelings.

Establish the Need: Use pictures to introduce a skill by having your students define the feeling and tell why they think it is that feeling. What happens when you put the wrong feeling with an expression? Discuss. Define facial expressions, gestures and body language.

Procedures:

Step 1: Model the skill:

A. Either model different faces or use pictures to describe different emotions.

B. Using "Think Aloud" strategies to understand the feeling:

(1) What feeling is the face showing? (2 Is it mad, glad, sad, afraid?

Helpful Hints: Some people don't show emotions on their faces. Talk about this and how you interpret the feelings of these people. Use body language with facial expressions.

Step 2: Role play with feedback:

A. Demonstrate interpreting different emotions from different students and then discuss.

B. When you don't understand facial expressions, what happens? i.e., mad from sad, nervous laughter from real laughter.

C. Role play simple facial expressions and have your students respond.

Helpful Hints: Make a list of some facial expressions that are difficult to interpret.

Step 3: Transfer training:

A. **School:** The principal walks in and smiles or has hands on hips and frowns. What is the feeling?

B. **Home/Community:** A parent is sitting with head resting on hands and not saying anything. What is the feeling?

C. **Peers:** A friend keeps turning away from you and doesn't answer you when you talk. What is the feeling?

Comments: The more time you spend with the person, the more you know their specific facial expressions and body language.

Extended Activities: Discuss feelings shown on TV. Use comics from newspapers, discuss body language. "Expressing My Feelings Award," page 58, "Homework Gram," page 32. Book: Cosgrove, Stephan. *The Gnome from Nome,* Los Angeles: Price Stern Sloan, 1974.

Lesson 15: Recognizing Other's Facial Expressions

1. What feeling is the face showing?

2. Is it mad, happy, sad, afraid?

FRIENDSHIP SKILLS

Expressing
My Feelings Award
to

_____

for using the skill of

_____

Date _____

Signed _____

Dennis Hanken, Ed.S. and Judith Kennedy, Ed.S.

Lesson 16: Starting a Conversation

Objective: Students will be able to start a conversation with people they do not know.

Materials Needed: Chalkboard, write "Think Aloud" strategies on the board or use a poster. Puppets. "Things to Try if You're Shy" on the following page.

Establish the Need: Discuss with your students that some people are very shy, and in order to develop friends, they may need to start a conversation with someone else. Discuss how you feel when you want to start a conversation, but you are not sure what to say. Use puppets to show starting a conversation. Define shy (hesitant to approach new situations).

Procedures:

Step 1: Model the skill:

A. Select a student with whom to model.

B. Model the skill using "Think Aloud" strategies:

> (1) Decide to approach the other person. (2) What will I talk about? (3) Look at the person. (4) Is the other person ready to listen? (5) Begin talking.

Helpful Hints: Ideas for conversations: what you did last weekend, current popular TV show or movie, current sport activity, what they did at recess.

Step 2: Role play with feedback:

A. Have your students brainstorm topics of conversation and write on the board. Assign your students in pairs. Instruct them to take turns starting a conversation. Rotate among the students and give feedback and correction.

B. More practice starting a conversation using "Think Aloud" strategies.

Helpful Hints: Have your students role play with one other student an example of inappropriate starting (i.e., while other person is busy, looking away, or monopolizing conversation). Elicit feedback from your students.

Step 3: Transfer training:

A. **School:** Assign your students the task of starting a conversation with someone in the lunch room. Report back.

B. **Home/Community:** Assign your students the task of starting a conversation with someone at home. Report back.

C. **Peers:** Assign your students the task of starting a conversation with friends at a game. Report back.

Comments: Students often have difficulty discerning if the time is right for starting a conversation. They may need practice on not interrupting. (Lesson 12)

Friendship Skills

Friendship Skills

Extended Activities: Observe your students at times when they start conversations and give correction and positive feedback. Ask other school staff to help reinforce this skill in the cafeteria, gym, and playground. "Friendship Award," page 55 and "Homework Gram," page 32.

Things to Try if You are Shy

Look at people's eyes when you are talking to them or they are talking to you. Looking in someone's eyes will help you listen better, and it helps people know you are interested in what they have to say. Looking at people helps you appear to be friendly.

Tell someone what you like about them or what they do. Tell a classmate you like his or her new coat, or the way he or she did math. Thank an adult for helping you.

Practice doing a favor for someone. Help someone by picking up something they dropped, hold a door for someone. And if you need help with something-ask for it!

Enjoy laughing with other people. (*Not* laughing *at* other people, though.) Everyone enjoys being around people who have developed a good sense of humor.

Be optimistic. Look for the good things in life. Expect that people will like you, and they are more likely to!

Lesson 16: Starting a Conversation

1. Decide to approach the other person.

2. What will I talk about?

3. Look at the person.

4. Is the other person ready to listen?

5. Begin talking.

FRIENDSHIP SKILLS

Lesson 17: Finishing a Conversation

Objective: Students will learn how to end a conversation in socially appropriate ways.

Materials Needed: Chalkboard, puppets.

Establish the Need: Ask your students if they have ever had someone walk off in the middle of their sentence. Elicit how that made them feel. With puppets demonstrate ending a conversation correctly using "Think Aloud" strategies.

Procedures:

Step 1: Model the skill:

A. With a student; model ending the conversation using "Think Aloud" strategies:

(1) Do I need to finish conversation? (2) Think about what to say. (3) Wait until the appropriate time. (4) Say it in a nice way.

Helpful Hints: Have your students come up with ideas for excusing themselves: (1) I'll be late for _____, sorry I have to go. (2) Excuse me. I have to meet someone now.

Step 2: Role play with feedback:

A. Pair students and instruct them to initiate and end a conversation.

B. Provide feedback and correction.

C. Assign your students to groups and have them, one at a time, practice leaving the group appropriately.

Helpful Hints: Activities for ending a conversation could include ending a game or a group activity. Have your students demonstrate ending a conversation inappropriately and elicit how that makes each person feel.

Step 3: Transfer training:

A. **School:** Assign your students to groups to play with at recess with instructions that each one will leave the group and join another. Report back.

B. **Home/Community:** Assign your students to end a conversation with a parent. Report back.

C. **Peers:** End a conversation with a child in your church or neighborhood. Report back.

Comments: Even adults have trouble ending conversations. This should be practiced and reinforced frequently.

Extended Activities: Auxiliary personnel could be informed of the Finishing a Conversation skill and asked to observe and provide feedback. Have a classroom social in which your students mingle, start a conversation, and end a conversation. "Friendship Award," page 55 and "Homework Gram," page 32.

Lesson 17: Finishing a Conversation

1. Do I need to finish the conversation?

2. Think about what to say.

3. Wait until the appropriate time.

4. Say it in a nice way.

FRIENDSHIP SKILLS

Lesson 18: Inviting Someone to Play

Objective: Students will learn how to ask someone to play with them.

Materials Needed: Puppets, stories "How to Be a Friend" and "A Friendly Face" on the following page.

Establish the Need: Read *I Want to Play* by Elizabeth Crary and discuss appropriate and inappropriate ways of inviting someone to play.

Read the stores on the next page and discuss.

Procedures:

Step 1: Model the skill:

Demonstrate how to ask others to play using "Think Aloud" strategies:

(1) Do I want to play? (2) How will I ask? (3) Look at them and ask. (4) Wait for the answer.

Helpful Hints: Times for asking are during free time, after school, recess, and weekends. When to ask is important (see "Interrupting," Lesson 12).

Step 2: Role play with feedback:

A. Your students role play asking a student to play a game with him or her.

B. Have them ask each other to play in an appropriate way. Give feedback.

Helpful Hints: Use puppets with your students, especially if they are shy. Have your students ask each other, but in a rude manner, for contrast. Are results different?

Step 3: Transfer training:

A. **School:** Ask someone during recess to play with you.

B. **Home/Community:** Ask a brother, sister, or parent to do an activity with you.

C. **Peers:** Ask a friend in the neighborhood to play.

Helpful Hints: There might be times when you want to play alone. You may also get some rejections when you ask others to play. See "Accepting No," Lesson 42.

Comments: Help your students know what to do if they are rejected. Choices might include: find something else to do, ask someone else to play, or do an activity by yourself.

Extended Activities: Practice how to handle rejections. Pass out board games, puzzles, or an art activity and have your students invite someone to do an activity with them. Observe periodically on the playground and compliment or assist someone in inviting someone to play. There are more interventions in *The Attention Deficit Disorders Intervention Manual* by S.B. McCarney on pages 42-43. "Friendship Award," page 55 and "Homework Gram," page 32.

How to Be a Friend

Be friendly to other people. People may think you are unfriendly when you're only shy. You don't have to wait for others to speak to you first; you can say "Hi."

Treat people the way you want to be treated. You can let your friend have the first turn, or do an activity that your friend wants to do some of the time. If you want to have friends, you need to be a good friend.

Listen and talk with your friend. Learn what he or she likes to do. Tell the other person about yourself. You can be a better friend if you really know the other person.

Do the things your friend likes to do at least part of the time.

When your friend tells you little secrets, don't tell them to other children. **Be a person other people can trust.**

Have fun and enjoy the things you do. No one likes to be around people who whine and complain. Develop a good attitude.

A Friendly Face

Jake was a new boy at school. His parents had moved here from another state. He was about average in sports, but he loved to play basketball. During recess one day, all the boys in the third grade were playing basketball. Jake stood nearby, but he was afraid to ask if he could join. Finally, Jake risked asking one of the boys if he could play too. The boy said, "Sure!" Jake found out all he had to do was ask.

Lesson 18: Inviting Someone to Play

1. Do I want to play?

2. How will I ask?

3. Look at them and ask.

4. Wait for the answer.

FRIENDSHIP SKILLS

Lesson 19: Joining in a Group Activity

Objective: Students will learn how to ask to join in a group activity.

Materials Needed: Chalkboard, playing cards, puppets, story on the next page.

Establish the Need: Joining in a group activity can be practiced every day, especially on the playground. Discuss being left out. This can be a sad time for someone. Sometimes being picked last is also a problem. Read the story "Jill Asks To Join an Activity" on the following page.

Procedures:

Step 1: Model the skill:

(1) Approach a person in the group. (2) Look at the person and smile. (3) Ask politely if I may join. (4) Wait for an answer.

Helpful Hints: Talk about taking risks. Discuss anxiety and rejection. Demonstrate by having three students play cards. "Think Aloud," "I'd like to play cards too, but I don't know these students very well. Of course if I don't ask, I'll be doing nothing" or start by saying, "Hi, what are you playing?" Wait for a response. "Could you use a fourth player," or "It looks interesting, could you show me how to play?"

Step 2: Role play with feedback:

A. Have your students take turns asking groups of three or four if they can join. Observe and give feedback.

B. Have your students practice until they feel comfortable. Other students can assist you to provide feedback.

Helpful Hints: This skill needs practice as much as possible. Some may never come to mastery in elementary school, but if they know how to attempt, this is helpful. Have a student force his or her way into a game and see what interaction takes place. Discuss the results.

Step 3: Transfer training:

A. **School:** Ask to join a group during recess or free time.

B. **Home/Community:** Ask to play a game with your family.

C. **Peers:** Ask to join a group in the neighborhood or park.

Comments: This skill needs lots of practice, both in and outside of school. Research shows that attempts to join in are more successful if the child hovers near the on-going activity before asking to join in (Dodge, Schlundt, Schoken, & Dehugack, 1983).

Extended Activities: Discuss fear and rejection. Transfer training activities are definitely needed to master this skill. Books: Crary, Elizabeth, *I Want To Play*. Seattle: Parenting Press, 1982. Bright, Robert. *Georgie and the Robbers*. New York: Doubleday, 1963. Cosgrove, Stephan. *Wheedle on the Needle*. Price Stern Sloan, Inc., 1975. Your counselor is a good resource.

Jill Asks to Join an Activity

Materials: Four puppets-Judy, Wendy, Jill, and Mac, or any names will do.

Jill doesn't know how to join a group activity.

JACK: Hi, gang, what should we do for recess today?

WENDY: I know, let's start a club with you, me, and Mac. We will pretend this cabin is our fort. We won't let anyone else in.

JACK: Hey, what about Jill-she may want to join.

WENDY: Too bad. She's still in the building.

            Later Jill arrives.

JILL: Hey, gang, this is my fort. So bug off. (She pushes Wendy and throws rocks at the fort).

            Jill stomps off crying.

MAC: Hi Wendy. Hi Jack. Is this the new club fort? What a great idea. What are all these rocks doing here?

WENDY: Jill came over and pushed me and threw rocks at our fort.

MAC: Was she mad at you?

JACK: I don't think so.

MAC: I'll go ask her.

MAC: Hey, Jill, neat fort that the club has-isn't it?

JILL: I have seen better.

MAC: I heard you threw rocks at it and pushed Wendy. What's your problem?

JILL: Well, they didn't want me to join and I wanted to play with them and join the club, but instead I got mad and threw rocks and pushed Wendy. I am really sorry.

Ask your students the following questions:

What did Jill mean by saying "this is my fort-bug off? (She really wanted to join the club but felt left out and got mad.)

Why do you think Jill pushed Wendy and threw rocks? (She was upset.)

Did you ever want to join a group, but felt rejected and said something or did something you didn't mean?

            Mac gives Jill some advice on how to join a group activity.

MAC: I know you're sorry. What you need is some help in asking to join a group.

JILL: What do you mean?

MAC:	When you see your friends doing something and you feel left out, instead of getting mad you need to go up to one of them and ask to join.
JILL:	What do you mean?
MAC:	Well, when you want to join the club with Wendy and Jack, you just go up to one of them, look at them, smile and ask to join.
JILL:	I didn't think pushing someone or throwing rocks would work.
MAC:	Exactly, then you should ask one person politely if you can join or play with them. Then wait for an answer. Usually if you act friendly the person will be friendly back.

Questions for your students:

What does Jill need to learn? (How to join in a group.)

What are the steps you take when you want to join? (Remember, go up to a person in the group, look at the person and smile ask to join in a polite way, wait for an answer.

Jill practices the skill.

JILL:	How do I ask politely or in a nice manner?
MAC:	Well, you could say, "Wendy, could I join the club and play in the fort?"
JILL:	Do you think that would work?
MAC:	Probably, if you ask in a friendly way, usually people are friendly back. How about trying it on Jack and Wendy?
JILL:	All right, I will at the next recess.

Wendy and Jack were playing in the club fort.

JILL:	(Looks at Wendy and says), "Can I join the club?"
WENDY:	Sure, we'd like you to join. We thought you were mad at us.
JILL:	Well, I was because I thought you didn't want me to play with you.

Friendship Skills

Questions for your students:

What were the results of Jill's asking to join? (Good. She was able to join the group without getting mad.)

WENDY: This is sure fun having Jill in the club, isn't it, Mac and Jack?

JACK: Yeah, this is a great club.

Questions for your students:

What was Jill's problem? (She didn't know how to ask to join the group.)

What steps did Mac teach Jill?

>   Go up to person in the group.

>   Look at the person and smile.

>   Ask politely if I may join.

>   Wait for an answer.

Have your students share some personal problems that occurred in their life when they tried joining in a group activity.

Lesson 19: Joining in a Group Activity

1. Approach a person in the group.

2. Look at a person and smile.

3. Ask politely if I may join.

4. Wait for an answer.

FRIENDSHIP SKILLS

Lesson 20: Playing a Game by the Rules

Objective: Students will learn to play a game by the rules, take turns in order, and wait patiently for their turn.

Materials Needed: Puppets.

Establish the Need: Ask your students if they have ever played a game where they are confused and rules keep changing. Does more arguing take place than fun? Discuss. Story with puppets, "Jordan's Basketball Game."

Procedures:

Step 1: Model the skill:

Demonstrate the steps for playing a game using "Think Aloud" strategies.

> (1) Know the rules. (2) Who goes first, next, and so forth. (3) Wait my turn.

Helpful Hints: (1) Discuss rules before you play. (2) Talk about who you follow. (3) Wait your turn and watch the game (paying attention).

Step 2: Role play with feedback:

A. Select a game which requires taking turns. Have your students create or simulate a game using "Think Aloud" procedures. Have them identify the steps. Give feedback.

B. Have your students practice playing cards with all the rules. Positive feedback.

Helpful Hints: Card and board games are good for this skill. Have your students play cards and not discuss the rules. See what happens when you don't discuss the rules. (Arguing and disorganization.) Give feedback.

Step 3: Transfer training:

A. **School:** Play softball, kickball, or a game with two or more players during recess. Follow the "Think Aloud" strategies.

B. **Home/Community:** Play a board game with your family.

C. **Peers:** Play hide and go seek in the neighborhood.

Comments: Two good skills to teach with this are "Losing Is Learning," Lesson 38 and "Wanting To Be First," Lesson 48.

Extended Activities: When children are fighting over games at recess, this would be a good skill to review. Book: Beatrice Schenk de Ringers. *How Joe the Bear and Sam the Mouse Got Together.* New York: Lothrop, Lee & Shephard, 1990. "Friendship Award," page 55 and "Homework Gram," page 32.

Jordan's Basketball Game

This is a story about Jordan and his friends playing a basketball game during recess. Ask the children to carefully (grades 2 to 3) choose students to play parts; (grade 1) have the older children play the roles of the puppets.

Materials:　　　　　　　　　Four Puppets-Jordan, Admiral, Shaq, Magic.

Jordan doesn't know how to follow rules of the basketball game.

JORDAN:	Oh, Great, there is Shaq, Admiral, and Magic playing basketball. I love that game.
ADMIRAL:	Oh, no! Here comes Jordan!
SHAQ:	No problem. He is a great player. Don't you like playing basketball with him?
MAGIC:	You'll see. He keeps the ball and doesn't always play by the rules.
JORDAN:	Hi guys! Basketball! Can I play with you?
ADMIRAL:	Well I guess so, we're playing HORSE. You are last and you have to wait your turn.
JORDAN:	What do you mean last. I'll start now. You guys know I won't miss. Watch!
SHAQ:	You have to follow me or you can't play.
JORDAN:	Follow you, are you kidding? The best always starts. You have to beat me then I'll follow you.
MAGIC:	You can't just bust in here and start playing by your own rules.
SHAG:	Besides, we were here first and started playing. If anyone joins us, they have to be last.
ADMIRAL:	Yeah, Man, you got to play by the rules.
JORDAN:	You guys and your rules. I'll take you all on and maybe I'll shoot left handed. I love this game.
MAGIC:	Jordan, take a hike. You just want your own way.
JORDAN:	Can you make this shot?
ADMIRAL:	Man, you are too much, nobody wants to play with you.
SHAQ:	Yeah, we don't even know whose turn it is now.
JORDAN:	Did you see that shot? WOW, am I good or what?
ADMIRAL:	We're history. So long, Jordan. We're going to shoot at another basket. Don't even bother coming along. You can't follow simple rules.

Educational Media Corporation®, Box 21311, Minneapolis, MN 55421-0311　　　　73

Friendship Skills

Questions for your students:

Why don't Shaq, Admiral, Jordan want to play with Jordan? (He doesn't follow the rules.)

How does Jordan make his friends feel? (Angry, upset, frustrated.)

Jordan's friends tell him about following rules.

JORDAN:	Fine, go ahead and leave, I'll just shoot baskets by myself. I love this game. I'll just shoot until I miss which I won't. (Pause) I guess this isn't much fun by myself. Maybe I'll go ask my friends if I can join their game.
SHAQ:	Not you again! You are not going to mess up our game.
JORDAN:	I am sorry. I know I blew it the last game. Could you give me another chance? I wasn't having any fun playing alone. I'll play by your rules if you teach me.
MAGIC:	You can learn the rules by watching us play.
ADMIRAL:	Right, then you can let us know when you know the rules.
JORDAN:	I can do that. I really want to play with you.
SHAQ:	And remember when you play with us, take turns and no "hogging" the ball.

Questions for your students:

Why does Jordan decide he doesn't want to play without his friends? (Not any fun.)

How do his friends teach Jordan to have fun playing HORSE? (Learn rules, watch others, take turns, ask to join.)

JORDAN:	You're right, This is more fun than playing alone.
SHAQ:	I am glad you're going to follow the rules and play with us.

Questions for your students:

How did Jordan's friend feel when he didn't follow the rules? (Upset, angry, wanted to play without him.)

What steps did Jordan's friends teach him?

Know the rules.

Who goes first, next, and so forth.

Wait my turn.

Discuss with your class what happens when children don't follow the rules of games.

Lesson 20: Playing a Game by the Rules

1. Know the rules.

2. Who goes first, next, and so forth.

3. Wait my turn.

FRIENDSHIP SKILLS

Lesson 21: Waiting Your Turn

Objective: Students will take turns in order and wait patiently for their turn during a game or activity.

Materials Needed: Puppets.

Establish the Need: Taking turns is an important rule of most games. We can't always be first. Discuss: if everybody takes turns and waits, then everyone gets an equal chance. Getting cuts is not fair. Read and discuss "Good Job, Fanny" on the following page.

Procedures:

Step 1: Model the skill:

A. Ask your students to identify some games that require taking turns.

B. Model, playing a card game using "Think Aloud" procedures:

(1) Determine who's first, i.e., flip a coin, guess a number. (2) Decide who's next, i.e., clockwise, alphabet, and so forth. (3) Wait for my turn. (4) Have fun.

Step 2: Role play with feedback:

A. Role play an activity where your students have to wait their turn.

B. Have your students role play an activity taking turns appropriately and give feedback. This helps the game go quicker and everybody seems to enjoy it more.

Helpful Hints: Suggested activity: During recess, you and a friend want to use one swing. Demonstrate what happens when you don't wait your turn. Rules are broken and chaos happens. Give feedback.

Step 3: Transfer training:

A. **School:** You wait your turn to play a game at recess. Report back.

B. **Home/Community:** You wait your turn in a game with your parents.

C. **Peers:** You wait your turn to play with a toy.

Helpful Hints: Some students call this "I am bored" while waiting to do something. See Lesson 35.

Comments: Every time you take turns in the classroom, emphasize fairness and lack of chaos.

Extended Activities: Corey, Dorothy. *Everybody Takes Turns*. Niles, IL: Albert Whitman & Co., 1980. Crary, Elizabeth, *I Want to Play,* Seattle Parenting Press, 1982.

Good Job, Fanny

Materials: Three puppets—Wally, Buddy, and Fanny.

Introduce the three puppets. Tell your students that you're going to present a story about these characters called "Good Job Fanny." Ask them to listen carefully.

Fanny doesn't know how to take turns.

WALLY: Uh-oh, Buddy, look. Here comes Fanny to play baseball with us.

BUDDY: Oh, no. It's no fun playing when she's here.

FANNY: Hi, Wally! Hi, Buddy! I just love to play baseball! Here I go!

WALLY: Fanny, you grabbed the ball away from me just as I was reaching for it.

FANNY: Oh, yes, isn't this fun?

WALLY: It isn't when you're around, Fanny, I'm going home.

FANNY: Why? It's lots of fun playing baseball, isn't it, Buddy?

BUDDY: No, Fanny. It isn't fun when you play. I'm going too.

FANNY: Wait! Don't go! I thought we were having fun together.

BUDDY: We don't have as much fun when you're here. Whenever you see someone pitching, you run up and grab the ball. You run bases with us, and you always want to hit. You don't take turns.

Ask your students:

Why don't Wally and Buddy like to play baseball with Fanny? (She doesn't take turns.)

How do they feel about Fanny not taking turns? (Bad, angry, not having fun.)

Wally and Buddy tell Fanny about taking turns.

FANNY: Okay, I'll take turns. What is "taking turns"?

WALLY: Taking turns is a way for everyone to get to play. We all like to be the batter, but the game is no fun if everyone bats and no one throws or catches.

BUDDY: Before we start playing, we decide when everyone will bat. We take turns. When we take turns, we determine who is first, decide who is next, wait for our turn, and have fun.

Ask your students:

What does Wally say "taking turns" means? (Everyone gets to play.)

How do we take turns? (Be sure the steps of the skill are mentioned.)

> Determine who is first.
>
> Decide who is next.
>
> Wait for my turn.
>
> Have fun.

Why do we take turns? (To be fair, to feel good about playing together.)

Fanny agrees to take turns.

FANNY:	How do I know when it's my turn?
BUDDY:	You need to ask who hits before you, and you can bat after they do.
FANNY:	But what do I do when someone else is batting the ball?
WALLY:	We take turns throwing, catching, and playing the bases. When you're not batting the ball, you can take a turn at third base.
BUDDY:	If you promise to wait your turn to bat, Fanny, I'll stay here and play.
FANNY:	But when will my turn be?
BUDDY:	We already agreed that Wally would bat after me. You can go after Wally.
FANNY:	Okay, I don't want everyone to go home. I'll play third base and wait for my turn to bat.
WALLY:	Fair enough, Fanny! Hooray for you!

Ask your students:

How do the boys feel about Fanny when she starts batting the ball without waiting her turn? How does deciding to take turns help Fanny? (She gets to bat the ball some of the time, and she also gets to play with Buddy and Wally because they like playing with her when she waits for her turn.)

What steps did Fanny learn? Review the skill steps, asking the children to repeat each one:

> Determine who is first.
>
> Decide who is next.
>
> Wait my turn.
>
> Have fun.

Lesson 21: Waiting Your Turn

1. Determine who is first.

2. Decide who is next.

3. Wait my turn.

4. Have fun!

FRIENDSHIP SKILLS

Lesson 22: Sharing

Objective: Students will learn rules for sharing equipment and toys.

Materials Needed: Story, "Little Red Hen," enough art supplies for four groups of children to share, markers and poster board.

Establish the Need: Read the story and discuss sharing work and outcomes.

Procedures:

Step 1: Model the skill:

With one or two students, model sharing markers to make a poster using "Think Aloud" strategies: (put on the chalkboard or use a poster)

(1) Gather the needed items. (2) Share the items. (3) Wait my turn. (4) Do something else while waiting. (5) Put the item back when done.

Step 2: Role play with feedback:

A. Divide your class into four groups and assign an art activity with each group getting only one box of crayons. Rotate and provide feedback.

B. Practice sharing in another art activity.

Helpful Hints: Your students may need help in brainstorming what to do while they wait. Role play with two to three students to see what happens if materials are not shared.

Step 3: Transfer training:

A. **School:** Ask the PE teacher to divide your students in groups and have them share equipment for a task.

B. **Home/Community:** Your students are asked to share the last popsicle (cookie, fruit, etc.) with a sibling.

C. **Peers:** Your students are asked to share equipment on the weekend. Report back.

Comments: This is an especially difficult task for the younger child and may take considerable practice.

Extended Activities: There are many classroom activities where you can build on sharing, to include: coloring, painting, playing ball, using a scissors, looking at books, cutting from magazines. "Friendship Award," page 55 and "Homework Gram," page 32.

Lesson 22: Sharing

1. Gather the needed items.

2. Share the items.

3. Wait my turn.

4. Do something else while I am waiting.

5. Put the item back when done.

FRIENDSHIP SKILLS

Lesson 23: Asking a Favor

Friendship Skills *(side margin)*

Objective: Students will ask a favor in a polite and positive way.

Materials Needed: Puppets.

Establish the Need: Is it difficult to ask for a favor? Use puppets to show asking a favor in a polite way. Discuss with your students that no one can do everything and each of us may need to ask for help from someone else at times.

Procedures:

Step 1: Model the skill:

A. Demonstrate asking a favor using "Think Aloud" procedures:

(1) Plan what to say, "Could you help me with this?" (2) Ask in a friendly way. (3) Say, "Thank you."

Helpful Hints: This skill is useful when borrowing objects from peers. Puppets may be used to make this practice more fun.

Step 2: Role play with feedback:

A. Have your students role play asking for a favor from another student.

B. Have your students ask for a favor, using the model above, in an appropriate manner. Give feedback.

Helpful Hints: Your students can use puppets. Have them ask for a favor inappropriately for contrast. Discuss the results.

Step 3: Transfer training:

A. **School:** Someone is making noise that interferes with your work or bothers you. What do you do?

B. **Home/Community:** The TV is too loud for you to do your homework.

C. **Peers:** A friend is going to the mall and you want to go also.

Helpful Hints: This takes time to be able to take the risk to ask someone to quit doing something in a nice manner. Have your students see they will get better results than from tattling or yelling.

Comments: The definition of a favor is anything a student needs help with, from problems with other people to school problems.

Extended Activities: Puppets. "Friendship Award," page 55 and "Homework Gram," page 32.

Lesson 23: Asking a Favor

1. Plan what to say.

2. Ask in a friendly way.

3. Say, "Thank You."

FRIENDSHIP SKILLS

Lesson 24: Complimenting

Objective: Students will select a person for complimenting and make a sincere compliment to the other person.

Materials Needed: Chalkboard. List of compliments. See extended activities.

Establish the Need: Ask your students to brainstorm why we compliment and how they feel when they receive a compliment (might include (1) making a person feel good, (2) wanting a person to like us, (3) showing we are friendly). Write the responses on the board.

Procedures:

Step 1: Model the skill:

Model using "Think Aloud" strategies:

(1) Decide what to compliment. (2) Decide on a time and place. (3) Give the compliment, (i.e., "You look nice." "I like your clothes." "You are a great friend.")

Step 2: Role play with feedback:

Assign students in groups of four, taking turns giving compliments. Students observe and offer feedback. Rotate among groups offering feedback.

Helpful Hints: Emphasis should be placed on sincerity. Have your students discuss the inappropriate time and place to compliment. Giving a compliment should result in a "thank you." (See the next lesson.)

Step 3: Transfer training:

A. **School:** Your students should compliment one staff member this week. Report back.

B. **Home/Community:** Your students should compliment one family member. Report back.

C. **Peers:** Compliment one other student at a game they played. Report back.

Comments: Sincere compliments are an important part of making friends. Model appropriate, sincere complimenting on a daily basis.

Extended Activities: Classroom work and relationships offer many opportunities to compliment students. Model this and praise students who compliment effectively. Compliment words: clever, friendly, fun, generous, helpful, honest, kind, smart, strong, good at... "Friendship Award," page 55 and "Homework Gram," page 32.

Lesson 24: Complimenting

1. Decide what to compliment.

2. Decide on a time and place.

3. Give the compliment, (i.e., "You look nice." "I like your clothes." "You are a great friend.")

FRIENDSHIP SKILLS

Lesson 25: Receiving a Compliment

Objective: Students will receive compliments by saying, "Thank you."

Materials Needed: Puppets.

Establish the Need: Discuss various feelings we may have when complimented. Discuss how you feel when receiving a compliment. Embarrassed, defensive, surprised, delighted, important, unsure. Stories, "Bob's Problem with Compliments" and "Nice Sweater," on the following page.

Procedures:

Step 1: Model the skill:

Using puppets and "Think Aloud" strategies: model receiving compliments.

> (1) Look at the person. (2) Listen. (3) Say "thank you."

Step 2: Role play with feedback:

A. Have your students in groups of four practice receiving compliments. Have the students who are observing give feedback.

B. Practice receiving compliments appropriately in groups. Rotate and offer feedback.

Helpful Hints: Students often feel embarrassed when receiving a compliment and may even become defensive. These students should be helped to accept compliments from others. Discuss receiving compliments poorly, i.e., bragging or disagreeing.

Step 3: Transfer training:

A. **School:** Ask school personnel to compliment your students this week on behavior, and so forth.

B. **Home/Community:** Send a note to parents asking them to help your lesson by complimenting their children.

C. **Peers:** Assign your students to report to class on compliments they received.

Comments: Research findings state that it takes five positive remarks to offset one negative one.

Extended Activities: Make more of an effort to sincerely compliment your students and watch for improvements in their accepting compliments.

Bob's Problem with Compliments

Bob was a student in a class for students with learning disabilities. He was there because he had a reading disability. However, Bob could do a lot of things better than most people. He was very good at doing math in his head, he was very fast, and he was quite good at fixing bikes.

Unfortunately, Bob had a problem in handling compliments. Sometimes after being praised or complimented, he would begin to brag about how good he was and how much better he was than others in the class. On other occasions, when he was praised, he would tell the person that they were wrong and that he was too dumb to do anything right.

While working on a math lesson one day, Mr. Carter, the teacher, complimented Bob for how quickly he was able to finish the problems. Bob said: "That's right! I'm the best! She (pointing to Judy) is the dumbest!" Of course, that started Judy and Bob in a name-calling contest, so Mr. Carter had to punish both of them.

On another day, Mr. Draw, the art teacher, complimented Bob for some art work he had just done. Instead of accepting the praise, Bob said the following: "It ain't any good. It looks like junk. I can't do anything right." Mr. Draw asked Bob to stay after school that day. Mr. Draw realized that Bob just needed to learn how to accept compliments.

Discuss the effect of bragging and self-depreciating comments. Discuss that bragging leads to social rejection and that depreciation of praise discourages further praise.

Nice Sweater

One day Karen was wearing a beautiful sweater her parents had given her. Jenny, her friend, noticed and said, "What a beautiful sweater!" Karen answered, "Thank you, Jenny, I really love it, too. You're the best friend I have ever had. You notice everything and always give me nice compliments."

Lesson 25: Receiving a Compliment

1. Look at the person.

2. Listen.

3. Say, "Thank You."

FRIENDSHIP SKILLS

Lesson 26: Telling the Truth

Objective: Students will distinguish truth from fantasy and tell the truth.

Materials Needed: Puppets, chalkboard. Stories: "Mercury and the Woodman," "The Shepherd Boy and the Wolf," or "What's a Friend to Do?" on the following pages.

Establish the Need: Read the story, "The Shepherd Boy and the Wolf." Discuss.

Procedures:

Step 1: Model the skill

A. Model using "Think Aloud" strategies that you have $5.00 in your billfold. Verify the statement by showing the money. Discuss the consequences of a lie. Does it feel better to lie or tell the truth?

B. "Think Aloud" strategies:

(1) Decide: Is it real or make believe? (2) Tell what is real.

Helpful Hints: Puppets: Use puppets to demonstrate telling the truth.

Step 2: Role play with feedback:

A. Have your students role play telling the truth to the class and verifying the statements.

B. Have your students tell another student the truth versus a lie. Discuss which feels better.

Helpful Hints: Use puppets. Talk about what happens when you tell a lie. Emphasize loss of trust. Have your students make up something to tell students which they can't verify. Discuss consequences of a lie. Point out to your students the loss of self-esteem that results from lying.

Step 3: Transfer training:

A. **School:** Have the principal ask your students how recess went.

B. **Home/Community:** Have your students tell their parents how the day went at school, the good and the bad, being truthful. Report back.

C. **Peers:** When the occasion arises, tell a friend that you broke or lost his or her toy. This is not easy to do.

Helpful Hints: Use puppets to help tell the truth when it may be uncomfortable, like breaking or losing something of value.

Comments: Talk about trust, the consequences of lying, telling a lie to cover a lie, worrying, the fear of being caught, a little white lie, and lying to get out of a situation.

Extended Activities: Have your students self-reward when they are honest ("Good for Me, I Told the Truth"). There are more interventions in *The Attention Deficit Disorders Intervention Manual* by S.B. McCarney on pages 62-63. "Homework Gram," page 32.

What's a Friend to Do?

What would you do if a friend asked you to help him cheat on a test? Suppose all you had to do was write big and not cover up your answers. What if no one would ever know? All you're really doing is helping out a friend...

Hold it! Your friend's biggest problem is not his schoolwork. It's the fact that he's planning to do something dishonest. And he wants you to be part of the scheme. Not only will you be cheating, but you'll be helping him lie to the teacher-telling her, through his test score, that he knows and understands things he doesn't. Then your friend will get even further behind.

Listen to your conscience, that voice inside you waving a red flag and telling you to stop. And don't be fooled into thinking no one will know. Even if you fool your teacher, *you* will know what you've done.

Take a deep breath, and tell your friend that you don't cheat. Then offer to help him study.

It's what a real friend does.

The Shepherd Boy and the Wolf

Every day the shepherd boy was sent with his father's sheep into the mountain pasture to guard the flock. It was, indeed, a lonely spot at the edge of a dark forest, and there were no companions with whom he could pass the long, weary hours of the day.

One day, just to stir up some excitement, he rushed down from the pasture, crying "Wolf! Wolf!" The villagers heard the alarm and came running with clubs and guns to help chase the marauder away, only to find the sheep grazing peacefully and no wolf in sight.

So well had the trick worked that the foolish boy tried it again and again, and each time the villagers came running, only to be laughed at for their pains.

But there came a day when a wolf really came. The boy screamed and called for help. But all in vain! The neighbors, supposing him to be up to his old tricks, paid no heed to his cries, and the wolf devoured the sheep.

Application: *Liars are not believed even when they tell the truth.*

Mercury and the Woodman

An honest, hard-working woodman was felling a tree on the bank of a deep river. In some way his hand slipped and his ax fell into the water and immediately sank to the bottom. Being a poor man who could ill afford to lose the tool by which he earned his livelihood he sat down and lamented his loss most bitterly.

But Mercury, whose river it was, suddenly appeared on the scene. When he had learned of the woodman's misfortune, he offered to do what he could to help.

Diving into the deep, swift-flowing stream, he brought up an ax made of solid gold.

"Could this be yours?" he asked.

"Alas, I wish it were," replied the woodman sadly.

Again Mercury dived into the icy-cold water and this time brought up an ax made of solid silver. But again the woodman shook his head and denied that the tool belonged to him. Mercury dived a third time and produced the identical ax which the man had lost.

Naturally the owner was delighted to see his trusty ax once more, and so was Mercury.

"You are an honest and a good man," said the messenger of the gods. "I want you to take the golden and the silver ax as a reward for telling the truth."

Thanking his benefactor, the woodman ran home to tell his wife of his good fortune. As the story spread, one of the neighbors rushed down to the same spot on the riverbank, threw his ax into the water, and began to moan and groan over his loss. Just as before, Mercury appeared, and learning what had occurred, dived into the water and fetched up a golden ax.

"Is this the ax you lost, my friend?" he asked.

"Yes, yes, that's it," lied the man, greedily reaching for the golden ax in Mercury's hand. But just as he was about to grasp the ax of gold, Mercury said: "Not so fast, sir. You are lying, and to punish you for not being truthful, I am not only denying you this, but I am leaving your own ax at the bottom of the river."

Application: *Honesty is the best policy.*

Lesson 26: Telling the Truth

1. Decide: Is it real or make-believe?

2. Tell what is real.

FRIENDSHIP SKILLS

Dennis Hanken, Ed.S. and Judith Kennedy, Ed.S.

Lesson 27: Saying You are Sorry

Objective: Students will apologize for mistakes or wrong doing which injures or infringes upon another person.

Materials Needed: Chalkboard, puppets, stories, "Even Best Friends Need to Apologize" and "Play Ball," on the next page.

Establish the Need: Knowing when to apologize helps maintain relationships and builds character. Using puppets, have one do something which hurts the other and then apologize. You could use a story on the next page.

Procedures:

Step 1: Model the skill:

    A. Create a scenario for apologizing (see Helpful Hints).

    B. Model the apology using "Think Aloud" strategies:

        (1) Did I hurt someone? (physically, emotionally) (2) Was it my fault? (3) Say I'm sorry.

Helpful Hints: Scenarios: (1) hit by a ball, (2) push somebody over, (3) call someone a name out of anger (4) dropped, broke friend's toy, (5) told friend's secret, (6) late for meeting.

Step 2: Role play with feedback:

    A. Have your students role play: bumping another student and apologize.

    B. Have one student call another a name. Apologize. Provide feedback.

Helpful Hints: Role play breaking another's pencil without apologizing. Talk about feelings and consequences when we do and do not apologize.

Step 3: Transfer training:

    A. **School:** You are late for Student Council. Apologize to the leader.

    B. **Home/Community:** You took your brother's shirt without asking and spilled on it.

    C. **Peers:** You had planned to treat a friend to a movie, but you have to go with your relatives instead. Apologize to friend.

Comments: What happens to you as a person when you don't apologize? Discuss how a person feels before apologizing (i.e., anxious, afraid) as well as how a person might feel receiving the apology (relieved, less upset). This may make your students more willing to try.

Extended Activities: Puppets to act out story (next page). School provides many opportunities to help students accept responsibility for mistakes and apologize. "Friendship Award," page 55 and "Homework Gram," page 32.

Even Best Friends Need to Apologize

Bill and Dennis were the best of friends. At Cloverdale Elementary School, everyone just assumed that if Bill was there Dennis would be close by. If they saw Dennis first, people would always ask why Bill was not with him. Both boys liked to have fun by playing tricks on each other. Once Bill took Dennis' pencil from his school box and replaced it with one that had erasers on both ends. After a good laugh, Bill gave Dennis his good pencil and they talked about that one for days.

Dennis' trick on Bill was just as much fun. He stuck a message on Bill's back that said "Call me Pete today!" Well it took Bill a long time to figure out why people were calling him Pete. He finally guessed that Dennis had played a trick on him. They had a good laugh and went on being best of buddies.

On a rainy day, Dennis decided to play another trick on Bill. Dennis took Bill's boots and filled them with water right before they went home from school. Bill didn't think that was funny at all. He couldn't get all the water out and his feet were wet all the way home. The next several days Bill wouldn't even talk to Dennis.

Dennis couldn't figure out why Bill was so angry for just a little trick like water in his boots. He asked Bill why he wouldn't be friends anymore. Bill told him that he was angry about having wet feet and wet socks. Instead of apologizing, Dennis laughed and told Bill he wasn't tough enough to take a little water. Unfortunately, that didn't help and Bill started to find new friends.

Poor Dennis had trouble making friends because he never would say he was sorry for any of his mistakes.

Play Ball

One day at school John hit a ball. The ball sailed over the fence and broke a window. Everyone ran away except John. He didn't know what to do; he was scared. One of his friends came back to him and said, "Let's go and apologize together." John calmed down and apologized to the owner. He also paid for the window. Accidents happen!

Lesson 27: Saying You are Sorry

1. Did I hurt someone?

2. Was it my fault?

3. Say "I'm sorry."

FRIENDSHIP SKILLS

Lesson 28: How to Help a Classmate

Objective: Students will learn when it is appropriate to offer help to another student.

Materials Needed: Props which could require assistance, i.e., books, ladder, film projector, puppets. Stories: "Jill and Sara" and "Stardust Is Too Busy To Help," on the following pages.

Establish the Need: Demonstrate trying to do something difficult like moving a long table; ask 2 to 3 students to assist you. Discuss the process with class. Story, "Jill and Sara." Puppets with story, "Stardust Is Too Busy To Help" (see the following pages).

Procedures:

Step 1: Model the skill:

A. Go over the steps with your students. Ask a student to move his or her desk and model offering help using the "Think Aloud" strategies:

(1) Does the person need help? (2) How can I help? (3) Ask the person. (4) Help.

Step 2: Role play with feedback:

A. Pair your students and have one offer to help the other with a difficult task. Discuss how they feel giving help.

B. Have students practice offering help while you rotate and give feedback.

Helpful Hints: The task could include packing a book bag, reaching an object, carrying objects and giving guidance when needed. Have your students role play taking a test and not offering to help each others.

Step 3: Transfer training:

A. **School:** Your students should offer help to someone in the lunchroom or hall. Report back.

B. **Home/Community:** Your students should offer help to someone in the family. Report back.

C. **Peers:** Offer help to a friend on a project. Report back.

Comments: Help your students to see that they should follow through on the help they offer.

Extended Activities: Encourage and point out opportunities to help out in your class. Give positive feedback to those who offer and help appropriately. Ask for help from the other staff in reinforcing the skill with your students. Book: Bridwell, Norman, *Clifford's Pals.* New York: Scholastic Inc., 1985. "Friendship Award," page 55 and "Homework Gram," page 32.

Jill and Sara

One day Mrs. Winter, the music teacher, assigned a music project to her class. Everyone had an assignment to practice a dance or song for the Christmas recital practice. The class members had to help each other by cooperating and being a good listener.

This worked very well for Sara. A friend of hers asked her to help sing and dance. When asked, Sara joined right in and helped sing with her partners and class. Her friend then helped Sara. Since Sara and her friend had some practice on the song, Sara's skit turned out to be the best in the class.

Jill was the best singer in Mrs. Winter's class, but she wasn't the best helper. Several classmates asked Jill to help, but she wouldn't because she knew she could sing the best song all by herself. She just did nothing while several class members worked on their routines. When they were done, Jill started to sing. When she realized that time was short, she began asking others to help, but nobody would. Jill's routine never got done and instead of being in the Christmas sing, Mrs. Winter just had to leave Jill's part out of the play.

1. Ask your students why it is important to help their friends. Make the point that we all need help occasionally and help has to be given to be received.

2. Ask your students to identify times when help probably should not be given. Elicit responses such as during tests, when the person is trying to get out of work, or when the child is directed to stay on his or her own task.

Stardust is Too Busy to Help

Materials: Five puppets-Angel, Stardust, Sunny, Moonglow, and Twinkles.

Use older students to present puppet play to first grade classes.

Ask everyone to listen to the puppet story.

ANGEL:	Stardust, where are you?
STARDUST:	What is it? I can't stop to talk; I am really busy.
ANGEL:	Could you just help me for a minute. I can't reach this broom. You're so much taller. I can't reach it please, oh, please.
STARDUST:	Sounds like a personal problem. I am in a hurry. Can't help you!
MOONGLOW:	Hi, Stardust could you please help me move this box. It is real heavy. I can't do it myself.
STARDUST:	Hey, get a life man. I am too busy to help you.
TWINKLES:	Hey, Stardust, could you please loan me $2.00? I'll pay you back tomorrow.
STARDUST:	Wish I could, but I am too busy. I have to go. See ya.

Questions for your students:

What are Twinkles, Moonglow, and Angel asking Stardust for? (Help them in a time of need.)

Why doesn't she choose to help them? (She is in a hurry.)

Stardust finds out she should have been more considerate and helpful.

SUNNY:	(Gloomy) Hey, Stardust.
STARDUST:	Sunny, I am here for our card game. What a day, I have been busy, busy!
SUNNY:	This was going to be a great day. I was going to have a slumber party. It was the last day of school. But Moonglow and Angel can't come because they didn't get their jobs done at home. Poor Twinkles lost her brother's $2.00 and got grounded.
STARDUST:	Oh! Gosh, are you telling me they were all on their way to your house?
SUNNY:	Well, I thought they wanted to come over. But they must have goofed off all day and they got in trouble. I still can't believe Twinkles couldn't have borrowed $2.00 from a friend.
STARDUST:	Oh! They wanted to come all right, but I was too busy to help them. Twinkles asked me for the $2.00 and I said no. Why didn't I help?

Questions for your students:

Why does Stardust feel bad? (She didn't stop to help.)

Have you ever chosen not to help someone? Did you make the right choice? What were your feelings?

Sunny tells Stardust how to offer help when someone is in need!

SUNNY: Being a friend means when your friend needs help you try to help them. If you are busy or in a hurry, you have to make a choice. Sometimes it only seems like we're busy, but you have to think of your friend. What would it be like if you needed help and someone said they were too busy to help you? If you help others, they will help you when you need it.

STARDUST: You're right. I was only thinking of myself. But it's not too late to plan for another slumber party. I will make sure that Angel, Moonglow, and Twinkles get help if they need it so they can come to the slumber party.

SUNNY: What are friends for? Helping each other is a precious part of friendship.

Ask your students:

Why didn't Stardust help her friends when they needed it?

How did she feel when she found out they couldn't come to the slumber party?

Why should friends help each other when they need it?

What are the "Think Aloud" strategies or Steps that Sunny is telling Stardust about?

Does another person need help?

How can I help?

Ask person?

Help

Discussion:

Talk about asking for help and not receiving help or about being too busy to help and then feeling bad about not helping.

This might be a good time to talk about recognizing social cues and others feelings.

Lesson 28: How to Help a Classmate

1. Does the person need help?

2. How can I help?

3. Ask the person.

4. Help.

FRIENDSHIP SKILLS

Lesson 29: Reacting to Teasing

Objective: Students will ignore, walk away, or change the subject when they are teased.

Materials Needed: Puppets, chalkboard, stories on the following pages.

Establish the Need: Show with puppets or pictures how people feel when they are teased. Ask your students to say the names people call each other and write on the board. Read and discuss story, "Amber," "Amy," or "Cora," on the following pages.

Procedures:

Step 1: Model the skill:

A. Using puppets model reacting to teasing. Write on the board "Think Aloud" strategies:

> What do I do when teased? (a) Ignore, (b) Walk away, (c) Change the subject.

B. Model each option dealing with teasing.

Step 2: Role play with feedback:

A. In threes have one student react to teasing from another while a third observes. Evaluate. Rotate roles. Your students should practice all three roles.

B. Practice appropriate reactions to teasing while you rotate and give feedback.

Helpful Hints: Have two students role play an inappropriate handling of teasing. Discuss the consequences.

Step 3: Transfer training:

A. **School:** Take your students to a playground and have them practice reacting to teasing.

B. **Home/Community:** Have your students report how they handled a brother or sister teasing and laughing at them.

C. **Peers:** Report a time you saw teasing in your own neighborhood.

Comments: Your students may need reminders that they may have to ignore for a long time before teasing will stop.

Extended Activities: (1) Have your students draw a poster showing how they feel when teased; then how they feel when they react to teasing by ignoring, walking away, or changing the subject. (2) Other school personnel can reinforce appropriate reactions to teasing. Stories. "Friendship Award," page 55 and "Homework Gram," page 32.

Dear Teacher:

I've got this problem. I have freckles on my face, legs, and arms. Everyone at school calls me "freckle face"! What should I do?

Amy

Dear Amy:

I love freckles. Of course, that's probably because I don't have to wear them on my nose every day. I'm sorry the kids tease you. No they probably won't stop-as long as they know it bothers you. "Freckle face" isn't such a terrible nickname, as nicknames go. It's not exaggerated or nasty. In fact, it's based on a biological fact-you do have freckles.

Nobody is totally happy with the way she looks. And if other kids pick up on that, they begin teasing you about whatever it is you don't like about yourself. In your case, that's freckles.

This is tough advice to follow, but it's the only solution to your problem: Ignore the "freckle-face" comments. When someone says, "You have freckles!? Laugh back and say, "You noticed!" Soon you'll find people aren't laughing at you, they're laughing with you.

Ms. Understanding

Dear Teacher:

I have to get glasses in a few months. I'm afraid that my friends will make fun of me. I mean, when my friend got a haircut everyone made fun of her. Just imagine what they're going to say to me! Can you help me?

Cora

Dear Cora:

Okay, let's imagine what they're going to say to you. They might call you "four-eyes" or "glasses face." But they might say, "Cute glasses!" or "Now that you can see to hit the ball, play on my team."

One thing is for sure-your classmates will notice, just like they noticed your friend's haircut. Anything new is always material for teasing or comment. But nothing stays new for long, and people usually get tired of teasing if it doesn't get much of a reaction.

So stop expecting the worst! Your glasses may make your eyes look bigger and prettier. Not only will your glasses make the world look better to you-they may make you look better to the world.

Ms. Glasses

Ask your students if they had ever been teased or called names. List some of the names they have been called on the chalkboard.

Amber

Amber was the meany of the school, at least that's what everybody said. She really wasn't such a bad person. Most of the time she got along well with everyone. The only times that she caused trouble were when the other children teased or called her names. When the children at school learned that she would get angry when called a name like "Pigtails" "Ding Dong" or "Weirdo": they called her names just to see what she would do.

Sometimes Amber would yell names back, sometimes she cried, and sometimes she even pulled hair and hit the other children. Whenever she got angry, she seemed to get into trouble. On the day she pulled Sara's hair, she was sent home. When she hit Billy Smith in the eye, she had to stay after school; and when she pulled Bob's ear, he hit her back and gave her a black eye.

Mrs. Grant, the school principal, decided that Amber had to learn how to deal with being teased. One day after school, Mrs. Grant and Amber practiced how to ignore teasing, by changing the subject and walking away. The next day some children tried to tease Amber but it didn't work. Amber just walked away or changed the subject. After about a week, the children began to see that Amber no longer got angry. Since it wasn't any fun to tease her, they stopped. The best part for Amber is that she no longer gets into trouble at school.

Lesson 29: Reacting to Teasing

What do I do when teased?

a. Ignore.

b. Walk away.

c. Change the subject.

FRIENDSHIP SKILLS

Lesson 30: Identify Your Feelings

Objective: Students will be able to identify their own feelings as they occur.

Materials Needed: Puppets, 3 x 5 cards. *Will need to put "Helpful Hints" on the 3 x 5 cards.

Establish the Need: Feelings are part of your personality. Identifying feelings is the first step to dealing with and expressing feelings. Discuss with your students why we need to identify feelings. Some students may fear this skill because they don't want to show their feelings. Story with puppets, "Samantha Learns About Feelings" on the next page.

Procedures:

Step 1: Model the skill:

    A. Discuss the feelings that occur on an everyday basis. Describe how you know when you are scared, happy, sad and so forth.

    B. "Think Aloud" strategies:

        (1) What am I feeling? (2) Does my body give me a clue? (3) How can I express this feeling?

    C. Decide what you would call the feeling. Say to yourself, "I feel..."

Helpful Hints: You could discuss blushing, tightening of stomach, and so forth, as physical sensations connected to feelings. Suggestions for 3 x 5 cards on feelings situations: (1) you lost a tooth, (2) you learned to read, (3) your friend hit you, (4) you lost a book, (5) your parents punished you for lying, (6) you moved to a new school, (7) your grandparents came from out of town to visit, (8) your brother/sister is sick, (9) you lost your jacket, (10) you had to stay in for recess, (11) you made a new friend, (12) you didn't get to go to the movie.

Step 2: Role play with feedback:

    A. Identify a physical symptom that might have feelings connected to it. Describe how you feel and identify it, i.e., fear.

    B. Use 3 x 5 cards with situations, pair your students and have them tell each other how they would feel in each situation. Why?

Step 3: Transfer training:

    A. **School:** Frustrated with a difficult assignment. How does your body feel? What can you do?

    B. **Home/Community:** Your parents forgot to do something with you that they promised. How do you feel?

    C. **Peers:** Your friend can't come over and play. How do you feel?

Comments: Develop a list of feelings. It is normal to have feelings. Reinforce appropriate expression of feelings. Your school counselor is an excellent resource on feelings.

Extended Activities: Stories (on the following pages), and puppets. Books: Riley, Susan. *Afraid (What Does It Mean?)* series. Elgin, IL: Child's World, Inc., 1978. Have your students cut pictures from magazines and make a collage of "Things That Make Me Happy, Sad, Afraid."

Samantha Learns About Feelings

Materials: 2 puppets-(Samantha shows fear and learns from it)

MOTHER: "Samantha," I thought you went to play at Amy's house.

SAMANTHA: No, I don't feel good.

MOTHER: I'm surprised. You seemed fine at breakfast.

SAMANTHA: Well, I have a stomachache.

MOTHER: Hmm, you've been sick the last several times Amy invited you over. What happens at Amy's house?

SAMANTHA: Well, Amy and I play with her dolls and have fun with her dress-up clothes, but then Brad comes home.

MOTHER: You're shaking and moving close to me. Do you know what you are feeling?

Ask your students:

What is Samantha feeling?

How do you know that?

Why do you think she is afraid?

MOTHER: Tell me what Brad does.

SAMANTHA: Well, he comes in and knocks our stuff over and yells at us.

MOTHER: I see. I guess I need to call Amy and Brad's mom. Hello, Mrs. Dunkshire, Samantha has been reluctant to come over because Brad scares her and I'm wondering what we can do. You'll talk to him? Good! I knew you would take care of things. Samantha, Brad's mom did not like hearing that he has been scaring you and Amy. She is going to talk to him right now.

SAMANTHA: Thanks, Mom! I feel better. Maybe I could call Amy and we could play.

Ask your students:

Why is it a good idea for Samantha to tell her Mother about this problems?

How is Samantha feeling now?

Lesson 30: Identifying Your Feelings

1. What am I feeling?

2. Does my body give me a clue?

3. How can I express this feeling?

EXPRESSING FEELINGS

Lesson 31: Showing Your Feelings

Objective: Students will identify feelings and choose how and when to express them.

Materials Needed: List of feelings, puppets, posters showing feelings.

Establish the Need: Use puppets to demonstrate expressing feeling mad, sad, afraid, and happy. Discuss various feelings and appropriate and inappropriate ways to expressing them.

Procedures:

Step 1: Model the skill:

A. Model skills using "Think Aloud" strategies:

(1) What am I feeling? (2) How do I want to express it? (3) What are the consequences? (4) Express the feeling.

B. Set up a hypothetical situation of seeing a big dog, going to a dentist, and so forth.

Helpful Hints: (1) Discuss physical sensations that go with different feelings. (2) Discuss how people deal with feelings: express them, exercise, walk away, talk with a friend. (3) Discuss inappropriate ways of dealing with feelings: fighting or hitting, stuffing feelings.

Step 2: Role play with feedback:

A. Give your students hypothetical situations and have them role play in groups of three with one sharing feelings, one listening, and one giving feedback. Rotate roles. Rotate and give feedback.

B. Have your students do more practice of appropriate expression of feelings.

Helpful Hints: Have your students show or discuss inappropriate ways of expressing feelings.

Step 3: Transfer training:

A. **School:** You are the last one picked for the game. How do you feel? How do you express these feelings?

B. **Home/Community:** Your brother or sister won't let you come into his or her bedroom. How do you feel? How do you express the feelings?

C. **Peers:** Your best friend ignores you at recess. How do you feel? How do you express those feelings?

Comments: It is important that students learn to identify sensations in their body associated with feelings (butterflies in stomach, heart beating fast) and to know that healthy expression of feelings is essential for physical and mental health.

Extended Activities: Scenarios that help elicit feelings: How do you feel when: It is going to snow, there is no school tomorrow, your cousin is coming, you're going shopping, your teacher keeps you in for recess, your friend is moving, you get picked for the team, you may move to another town, your sister has your favorite toy.

Lesson 31: Expressing Your Feelings

1. What am I feeling?

2. How do I want to express it?

3. What are the consequences?

4. Express the feeling.

EXPRESSING FEELINGS

Lesson 32: Recognizing Another's Feelings

Objective: Students will be able to recognize other people's feelings by observing facial expressions and posture.

Materials Needed: Puppets, story.

Establish the Need: Recognizing another's feelings helps establish personal boundaries and helps you become more socially adept. Discuss how important it is to be able to recognize other's feelings. What happens when you can't? (Embarrassment, anger, defensiveness, misunderstanding, and so forth) Demonstrate anger and help your students see how you know it is anger. What happens after you know? Read the story, "Sarah Learns About Feelings," on the following page.

Procedures:

Step 1: Model the skill:

A. Review the list of feelings.

B. Choose a feeling and do not tell your class. Demonstrate it to your class. Have them look at the facial expression and body posture and try to guess the feeling using "Think Aloud" strategies:

> (1) Watch the person. (2) Name the person's feeling. (3) Choose a response: a) Ask the person about the feeling. b) Walk away. c) Comfort the person.

Step 2: Role play with feedback:

A. Demonstrate using "Think Aloud" techniques acting out several feelings.

B. Have your students recognize more feelings from adults and other students.

Helpful Hints: Your students might find it easier to recognize others' feelings if they know that person well. Discuss when you might decide to not ask what the person is feeling.

Step 3: Transfer training:

A. **School:** After assignments are handed back, one student begins to cry. What is the student feeling?

B. **Home/Community:** Mom or dad are slamming doors and muttering to himself or herself.

C. **Peers:** A friend ignores you for most of the day.

Helpful Hints: Use feelings that happen on a daily basis. Do not try to identify ones that are seldom seen.

Comments: Body posture and facial expressions may vary from person to person, but your class should pick up on common signs. Try varying activities from students to adults. Also, don't forget tone of voice.

Extended Activities: Puppets, pictures depicting feelings.

Sarah Learns About Feelings

Materials: 5 puppets

Introduce the puppets and the story. This story is about a girl named Sarah who learns to recognize what someone else is feeling.

SARAH: I like it when you take me for walks in the park, Emily. This is fun.

EMILY: I like it too. Look, there is Robert. How are you doing, Robert?

SARAH: Robert isn't answering. He is walking along with his head down, shoulders stumped, and feet dragging. What's up with him?

EMILY: I think Robert is feeling sad. Doesn't his face look sad? Robert, we're talking to you.

Ask your students:

How does Robert feel? (Sad)

How can you tell? (Body posture, expression on face)

SARAH: Well, let's go on, Emily. I want to go down the slide. Look! There is Jan.

EMILY: Look at her go down the slide her hands in the air, laughing. What kind of an experience do you think she is having?

Ask your students:

How is Jan feeling? (happy)

How can you tell? (laughing, having fun)

SARAH: Whew, I liked the slide, but I'm tired of that. Lets go to the paddle boars. Hey, look, there is Greg.

GREG: Gosh, darn, I lost my cotton candy in the lake. I leaned over to look at a stupid fish, and the candy fell off the stick. (Stomps his feet, scowls and kicks dirt.)

EMILY: Looks like Greg has a problem. What do you think, Sarah?

Ask your students:

How does Greg feel? (angry)

How can you tell? (stomping, kicking, scowling)

EMILY: Well, you saw a lot of people today, Sarah. Did you learn anything?

SARAH: Yes, I learned to watch the other person to figure out what I think they are feeling, then to name the feeling, and last to choose how I want to respond to their feeling.

Lesson 32: Recognizing Another's Feelings

1. Watch the person.

2. Name the person's feelings.

3. Choose a response:

a. Ask the person about the feeling.

b. Walk away.

c. Comfort the person.

EXPRESSING FEELINGS

Lesson 33: Showing Concerns for Another's Feelings

Objective: Students will name feelings and offer support to friends who have a problem.

Materials Needed: Puppets.

Establish the Need: Using puppets, demonstrate two friends: one with a problem and the other responding supportively. Discuss the feelings portrayed.

Procedures:

Step 1: Model the skill:

A. With a puppet and using "Think Aloud" strategies, model an appropriate response to a friend with a problem. Discuss.

B. "Think Aloud" strategies:

(1) Name the other person's feeling. (2) Choose a response: a) Ask if a person feels that way. b) Walk away-deal with the person when less angry c.) Ask if I can help.

Helpful Hints: Review the feeling pictures in Lesson 34 to help your students identify feelings.

Step 2: Role play with feedback:

A. Put your students in groups of three. Have one student share a problem, one student respond, and the third student evaluate. Rotate roles. Rotate and give feedback.

B. More practice with appropriate concern for another's feelings.

Helpful Hints: Ideas for role play: (1) A student struggling with an assignment. (2) A student whose family member is having surgery. (3) A student just won a trophy in a sport. (4) A student whose bike was stolen. Have your students role play inappropriate response to another's feelings and discuss the feelings of the people involved.

Step 3: Transfer training:

A. **School:** Elicit help from other school personnel to model showing concern and reinforcing students who show concern for others.

B. **Home/Community:** Write a note to parents citing the skill we are working on. Ask them to model and reinforce.

C. **Peers:** Watch for opportunities to reinforce your students and model the behavior for showing concern for another's feelings.

Comments: Empathy is an important personal skill which will not always have been modeled for your students. Use every opportunity to teach and reinforce this skill.

Extended Activities: (1) Visit a nursing home where your students can interact with people who are facing that stage in life. (2) This is an excellent skill to increase empathy for people who are physically or cognitively challenged or racially different. Involve the disabled students in your class and model and reinforce empathy.

Lesson 33: Showing Concerns for Another's Feelings

1. Name the other person's feelings.

2. Choose a response:

a. Ask if a person feels that way

b. Walk away-deal with the person when less angry.

c. Ask if I can help.

EXPRESSING FEELINGS

Lesson 34: Seven Common Emotions

Objective: Students will be able to list, recognize, and express seven common emotions: (Anger, fear, frustration, affection, worry, loneliness, sullenness).

Materials Needed: Chalkboard, puppets. (It may take several days to cover all 7 emotions.) Pictures depicting various feelings.

Establish the Need: Show pictures depicting feelings. Have your students identify the feeling of each and discuss situations that might evoke that feeling. Tell them all feelings are okay, but how we express those feelings sometimes causes problems. Give some examples of these problems.

Procedures:

Anger

Fear

Frustration

Affection

Step 1: Model the skill:

A. Demonstrate each feeling with posters using "Think Aloud" strategies and emphasize facial expressions and body language.

B. "Think Aloud" strategies:

(1) What am I feeling? (2) What clues does my body give. (3) Name ways I can express the feeling. (4) Choose.

Helpful Hints: Feelings evoke some fairly universal body symptoms that can assist children in identifying an emotion, i.e., **ANGER** = red face, clinched hands; **FEAR** = butterflies in the stomach, sweating hands; **FRUSTRATION** = tight jaw, curled brow; **AFFECTION** = warm feelings in stomach/chest; **WORRY** = tight, upset stomach; **LONELINESS** = empty feeling in chest; **SULLEN** = wrinkled brow.

Step 2: Role play with feedback:

A. Have your students role play each feeling using tone of voice, posture, and facial expression. Elicit feedback.

B. Discuss why it is important to have ways of dealing with each feeling appropriately versus inappropriately.

C. List positive alternative ways to express each feeling.

Helpful Hints: (1) What are some physical symptoms of **ANGER?** What are some of the things that make you angry? Name some ways to express anger. (2) What are some physical symptoms of **FEAR?** What are some of the things that scare you? How do you express your fear? What things do you do to keep yourself safe? (3) What are the physical symptoms of **FRUSTRATION?** What frustrates you? How do you act when frustrated? What other ways could you express frustration? (4) **AFFECTION:** a) How is affection given at home with words? b) This is a good time to talk about good touch and bad touch. The counselor is an excellent resource for this. c) How can you show affection at school with peers and adults? (5) **WORRY:** a) What makes you worry? b) What are physical symptoms of worry? c) Ask someone what worrying will accomplish? d) Be proactive instead of reactive, i.e., what might you do to stop worrying? f) Talk about it.

Worry

Puzzled

Grouchy

(6) **LONELY:** a) What is being lonely? b) Describe physical symptoms? c) What are some things you can do when lonely? d) Some people like to be alone. e) Describe the feeling using "Think Aloud" strategies. f) It is okay to feel this way; it usually passes. (7) **SULLENNESS/GROUCHY:** a) What is being a "grouch"? b) What are the physical symptoms? c) Do you like being "grouchy"? d) Can you change the way you feel? e) Do you want to change the way you feel? f) What made you "grouchy"? g) Does talking about it help.

Step 3: Transfer training:

A. **School:** What do you do when: (1) You are afraid to take a test? (2) You are mad at your teacher? (3) You can't figure out a math problem? (4) You want to hug your teacher, but you didn't know how to approach him or her? (5) You always worry about "flunking" a test? (6) Sometimes you think others don't care about you? (7) Sometimes you wish you could stay in bed and not talk to anyone at school?

B. **Home/Community:** What do you do when: (1) You are afraid to stay at home alone? (2) You are angry at your mother or father? (3) Your brother or sister is playing with your toy? (4) Your father kisses you at bedtime and you don't know how to ask him to stop? (5) You worry about mom and dad? (6) When everyone is gone it seems very lonely? (7) Everyone in the house seems to be doing things all wrong?

C. **Peers:** What do you do when: (1) You are afraid to go out at recess because a boy is going to beat you up? (2) You are upset with your friend? (3) Your friend has trouble joining in groups with you? (4) Your friend is always touching you and it "bugs" you? (5) You worry about losing a friend? (6) When you can't find anyone to play with, it seems like a lonely world? (7) If my friend would only agree with me, there would be no need to be angry?

Comments: This may take seven or more weeks to cover using one week per feeling.

Extended Activities: Puppets, plays to act out each feeling. "Iktomi" plays address these feelings and can be acquired from Indian Education or the library. Counselors are excellent resources for helping students identify and deal with feelings.

Lesson 34: Seven Common Emotions

1. What am I feeling?

2. What clues does my body give?

3. Name ways I can express the feeling.

4. Choose.

EXPRESSING FEELINGS

Lesson 35: Overcoming Boredom

Objective: Students will be able to identify when they are bored and make choices of acceptable activity.

Materials Needed: Chalkboard, activity, Learning Centers.

Establish the Need: Discuss with your students when they might be bored: no one to play with, long math sheet not done, and so forth. Brainstorm with your class acceptable activities when assigned work is completed.

Procedures:

Step 1: Model the skill:

Model feeling bored and finding something to do using "Think Aloud" strategies: (1) Recognize I'm bored. (2) Am I done with my work? (3) What else can I do? (4) Find something to do. (There will need to be activity learning centers available.)

Helpful Hints: Discuss physical symptoms: restless, angry, upset, worried, agitated, demanding, impatient, jittery.

Step 2: Role play with feedback:

A. Establish a scenario when a student is bored, group students in 4s and have them role play, taking turns identifying boredom and choosing something to do.

B. Have your students continue practicing appropriate choices. Rotate and provide feedback.

Helpful Hints: Possible scenarios: (1) Don't want to play any game available on the playground/no one around to play with; (2) Worksheet is long and you're tired of doing it. (3) Didn't get sufficient sleep last night; (4) You are having trouble completing a worksheet. For contrast select three students to role play inappropriate choices to being bored, i.e., bugging others, going to the bathroom, talking out loud, disturbing class, getting into trouble.

Step 3: Transfer training:

A. **School:** Your students are assigned tasks of identifying time when they are bored, choosing something to do and reporting to the class.

B. **Home/Community:** No one is around on Saturday, you are bored, what do you do?

C. **Peers:** All the equipment for playground is already checked out; what do you and a friend do?

Comments: Your students will need to be taught that you can't leave work undone, but can do some activity (stretching, going to get a drink, laying head on desk for one minute, etc.) and then return to work. Having Learning Centers set up which students enjoy can be great motivators for completing work.

Extended Activities: Have each student generate his or her own packet of acceptable activities to do when done with seat work. Your class could assemble packets of acceptable activities to do when bored. "Dealing with Stress Award," page 120 and "Homework Gram," page 32.

Lesson 35: Overcoming Boredom

1. Recognize I'm bored.

2. Am I done with my work?

3. What else can I do?

4. Find something to do.

RELIEVING STRESS

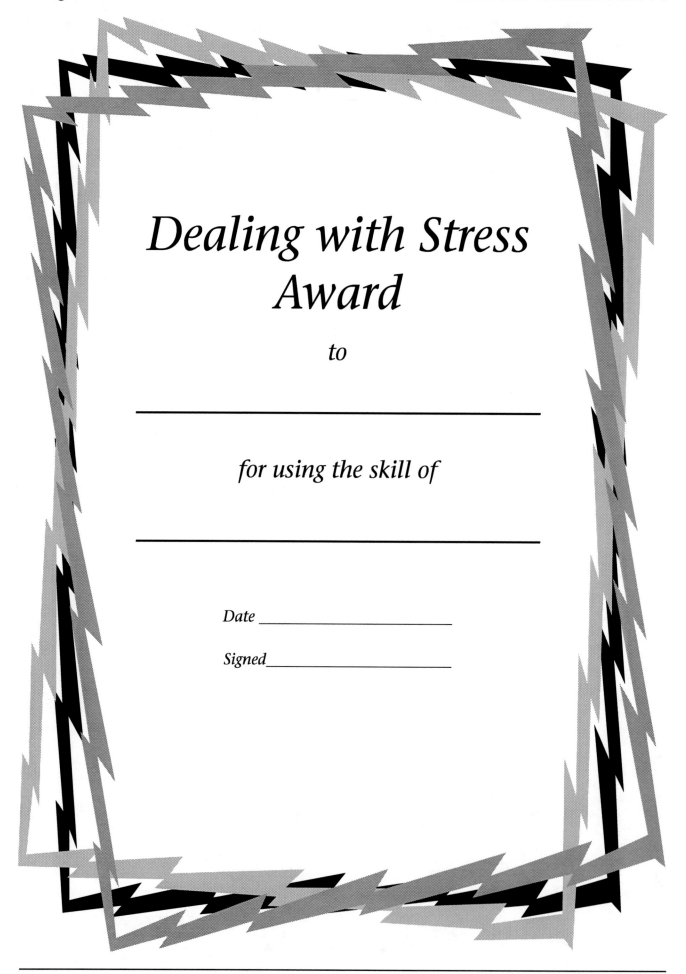

Dealing with Stress Award

to

_____

for using the skill of

_____

Date _____

*Signed*_____

Lesson 36: Stating a Complaint

Objective: Your students will be able to make a complaint to adults and peers.

Materials Needed: "Cinderella," chalkboard.

Establish the Need: Read "Cinderella." Ask your students if Cinderella was treated fairly. What might she have done about it?

Procedures:

Step 1: Model the skill:

A. Model making a complaint using "Think Aloud" strategies:

(1) Decide if a complaint will do any good. (2) To whom will I make a complaint? (3) Stand up, look at the person and use a strong voice. (4) Keep trying until you get an answer.

B. Complaint could include getting wrong product, people cutting in line, someone taking your parking spot, and so forth.

Step 2: Role play with feedback:

A. Brainstorm some "lead-ins" for making a complaint. Establish some scenarios: someone takes the swing, ball, and so forth. Your teacher gives everyone a paper, but you. The principal blames you for something you didn't do. Group students in 3s and 4s and have them alternate practice with feedback.

B. Make a complaint appropriately and discuss.

Helpful Hints: Lead in's: (1) "Excuse me, but I had the swing first. (2) I wish to make a complaint. (3) I have a problem and would like your help with it." For contrast answer a complaint with anger or defensiveness. Discuss the results.

Step 3: Transfer training:

A. **School:** Ask the principal to let your students practice with him or her in making a complaint. Familiarize the principal with the skill steps.

B. **Home/Community:** Write a note to the parents describing the skill and request their reinforcement of making a complaint. Report back.

C. **Peers:** Assign your students to make a complaint to a friend at home and report back.

Comments: This is a difficult skill and it requires considerable practice for students, especially when complaining to an adult. Assertiveness training techniques are appropriate here.

Extended Activities: Honor students' rights to make a complaint in the classroom. Reinforce appropriate complaint making. You may want to discuss the difference between making a complaint and constantly complaining, whining, or tattling. This would be a good time to talk about fairness and what it is to be fair. "Dealing with Stress Award," page 120 and "Homework Gram," page 32.

Lesson 36: Stating a Complaint

1. Decide if a complaint will do any good.

2. To whom will I make a complaint?

3. Stand up, look at the person, and use a strong voice.

4. Keep trying until I get an answer.

RELIEVING STRESS

Dennis Hanken, Ed.S. and Judith Kennedy, Ed.S.

Lesson 37: Answering a Complaint

Objective: Your students will listen to the complaint, ask questions if needed, decide if it is justified, and choose a response.

Materials Needed: Puppets, prepared 3 x 5 cards containing complaints (under helpful hints).

Establish the Need: Discuss with your students incidences when others may have reason for a legitimate complaint with them. Give examples of behaviors a person might do in class that would bother other people. Elicit a student response to complaints about their behaviors in the class that might bother others.

Procedures:

Step 1: Model the skill:

Model appropriate skill of answering a complaint using "Think Aloud" strategies:

(1) Is the complaint justified? (2) How do I want to respond? a) apologize, b) explain my behavior, c) suggest what I can do.

Step 2: Role play with feedback:

A. In groups of 3 or 4 have your students role play responses to complaints on cards. Have the other students evaluate. Rotate and give feedback.

B. More role playing of appropriate answers to complaint.

Helpful Hints: 3 x 5 card complaint suggestions: (1) Friend is waiting to walk home with you. When you come out friend says, "You took too long! I should have walked home myself." (2) You use mom's comb and don't put it back. Mom says, "I can't find my comb! Have you had it again?" (3) In activity at recess friend complains, "You haven't shared the jump rope. You are a rope hogger!" Have your students role play some inappropriate responses to a complaint. Give feedback.

Step 3: Transfer training:

A. **School:** Ask the school personnel to challenge your students in situations at school and give feedback to the way they answer the complaint.

B. **Home/Community:** Write a note to parents describing the skill and ask them to do two practice complaints with their child. Report back.

C. **Peers:** This week each student is to report how he or she handled a complaint from another child.

Comments: It is important to teach your students that defensiveness is common, but not desirable.

Extended Activities: (1) There are numerous occasions in class where you can point out mistakes of a child and help him or her answer that complaint in an appropriate manner. You can be a good model for giving and receiving complaints. "Dealing with Stress Award," page 120 and "Homework Gram," page 32.

Lesson 37: Answering a Complaint

1. Is the complaint justified?

2. How do I want to respond?

a. Apologize.

b. Explain my behavior.

c. Suggest what I can do.

RELIEVING STRESS

Lesson 38: Losing is Learning/ Showing Sportsmanship

Objective: Students will be able to deal with losing appropriately and show good sportsmanship.

Materials Needed: Puppets.

Establish the Need: There will be times in your life when you can't always win. Losing is a part of life. You can lose graciously and be proud of your behavior. Use the puppets with the story, "Big Daddy Helps His Friends," on the following page.

Procedures:

Step 1: Model the skill:

Model using "Think Aloud" strategies losing at an activity:

(1) Say "congratulations" to the other team. (2) Smile. (3) Shake hands.

Helpful Hints: Discuss relaxation techniques (Lesson 44). Both winner and losers should tell each other "good game."

Step 2: Role play with feedback:

A. Your students should role play in groups of five losing a game using "Think Aloud" strategies. Rotate roles.

B. Then have them demonstrate losing a game, shaking hands, and talking about their efforts.

Helpful Hints: For contrast, have your students gripe and whine after losing a game. Stomp off and get mad. Give feedback.

Step 3: Transfer training:

A. **School:** You lose a group game during recess.

B. **Home/Community:** You lose a game with your brother or sister.

C. **Peers:** You lose a game with best friend.

Helpful Hints: It is really difficult for some people to lose. There is poor role modeling for this on TV, and so forth.

Comments: Ask your students what they do when they lose. Make a list. How do you feel when you lose/win?

Extended Activities: Puppets. Story: Crary, Elizabeth, *I Want To Play*. Seattle: Parenting Press, 1982. "Dealing with Stress Award," page 120 and "Homework Gram," page 32.

Big Daddy Helps His Friends

Materials: Three puppets-Rocket Man, Speedy, and Big Daddy.

Have your students volunteer (2 to 3 grade). Older students may want to help with grade 1 students.

Rocket Man rubs it in when he wins, and Speedy doesn't know how to act when she loses.

Rocket Man:	I am the best, I won by a landslide. You call yourself Speedy? Why you're slower than slow. I am so fast I could probably beat any high school student.
Speedy:	You know you cheated. You said you would give me a half-block head start and you only gave me half of that. Man, you must really like to win to cheat that much.
Rocket Man:	Girl, I won fair and square. You just don't like to lose the championship race of the neighborhood.
Big Daddy:	Take a breather you two. You're going to wake up the neighborhood. I like you both, but can't you figure this out without yelling and arguing?
Speedy:	I hate to say this, but this doesn't concern you. So bug off!
Rocket Man:	Yeah, mind your own business.
Big Daddy:	You know, you two are acting like three year olds. I want to help you handle this problem. Tell me what happened.
Rocket Man:	Well, I said I was the fastest boy in the neighborhood and Speedy said she was the fastest girl. Well, I told her I could beat her in a race around the block even if I gave her a half block head start. She said I only gave her half that much of a head start. She said I cheated.
Speedy:	Well fair is fair. He cheated and he is the biggest sack of wind I know.
Big Daddy:	Wow, you two need to learn how to win and lose.

Questions for your students:

What was the problem between Speedy and Rocket Man?

Explain what it is to be a good loser or a good winner?

Should you expect to win every time you play a game or get in a race?

Relieving Stress

Big Daddy helps Rocket Man and Speedy to compromise.

Rocket Man: I am a good winner.

Speedy: I still think I should have won.

Big Daddy: Rocket Man, when you won the big race, what did you want Speedy to do?

Rocket Man: I wanted her to say, "you are really fast—good race." She could shake my hand and tell everyone how fast I am.

Big Daddy: What did you want Rocket Man to say to you after the race.

Speedy: Well, I didn't want him to rub my nose in it and gloat and pretend he's the fastest man alive. He could have said, "You can run really fast, good race!"

Big Daddy: So each of you had some good thoughts about what each other could say! No time like the present, say them now!

Rocket Man: Speedy, you ran a great race. I am sorry you lost.

Speedy: You are a great runner. Even though I had a head start I still couldn't catch you. (SMILE) You are definitely a faster runner than I am.

Big Daddy: Good job! Are you friends or are you going to let some dumb race come between you?

Friends to the end.

Questions for your students:

What was the result of the way Speedy and Rocket Man treated each other after the race? (Both showed poor sportsmanship and feelings were hurt.)

What does it mean to be a good winner?

> Say "Thank you" or something nice when congratulated.
>
> Smile and shake hands.
>
> Say something to other player that will make them feel good about himself or herself.

What does it mean to be a good loser?

> Say "congratulations."
>
> Smile.
>
> Shake hands.

Discuss what the purpose of competition is. "Trying When It's Hard" is a good topic. (Lesson 13) Some people are better at sports than others because of natural athletic skills. Should they act better than others? Discuss why TV doesn't always help us find good role models in sports. Discuss what Charles Barkley said, "I am not a role model, I just play basketball. I don't want people to look up to me as a positive role model."

Lesson 38: Losing is Learning/ Showing Sportsmanship

1. Say "congratulations" to the other team.

2. Smile.

3. Shake hands.

RELIEVING STRESS

Lesson 39: Dealing with Being Excluded

Objective: Students will consider other options when feeling left out.

Materials Needed: Chalkboard, story *The Ugly Duckling*. How did the Ugly Duckling deal with being excluded? What other choices might he have made?

Establish the Need: Ask your students how they would feel if everyone in class was invited to a party except for them. (Feelings of anger and hurt are normal.)

Procedures:

Step 1: Model the skill:

Set up a scenario and model being left out of a game using "Think Aloud" strategies:

(1) Why am I feeling left out? (2) What do I want to do about it? a) Ask to join. b) Find something else to do. (3) Choose the best one.

Step 2: Role play with feedback:

A. In pairs have your students practice being left out, giving each other feedback. Rotate and provide feedback.

B. More role play practice of appropriate action when left out.

Helpful Hints: Possible activities to be excluded from a: (1) game, (2) party, (3) meeting, (4) play, (5) talking. Role play inappropriate responses to being left out. Discuss.

Step 3: Transfer training:

A. **School:** Alert the playground staff to the skill being taught and ask them to reinforce the children who deal with being excluded.

B. **Home/Community:** Ask a student to report how he or she handled being left out by brothers or sisters.

C. **Peers:** How would a student handle being left out of a neighborhood party?

Comments: Helping your students to deal with this in a positive manner will equip them with a skill they will need throughout their lives.

Extended Activities: "Dealing with Stress Award," page 120 and "Homework Gram," page 32.

Relieving Stress

Lesson 39: Dealing with Being Excluded

1. Why am I feeling left out?

2. What do I want to do about it?

a. Ask to join.

b. Find something else to do.

3. Choose the best one.

RELIEVING STRESS

Lesson 40: Handling Embarrassment

Objective: Students will be able to take action when they feel embarrassed.

Materials Needed: Humorous pictures, homework, chalkboard.

Establish the Need: If you can laugh in embarrassing situations, it is usually not as bad as it seems at the time. Have your students talk about embarrassing moments and what happened!

Procedures:

Step 1: Model the skill:

A. Make a list of embarrassing moments.

B. Demonstrate an incident using "Think Aloud" steps: (facial expression, posture, tone of voice, etc. Discuss the steps: What is the worse thing that can happen when you are embarrassed?)

C. "Think Aloud":

(1) Am I embarrassed? (2) What caused it? (3) Consider options: a) Ignore it. b) Change the topic. c) Reassure self. (4) Choose an action.

Helpful Hints: Spilling water on front of pants, failing a test, spilling food on themselves, receiving an insult, being teased about boyfriend, tripping.

Step 2: Role play with feedback:

A. Ask your students to select a situation and role play in front of the class. Give feedback.

B. Create a situation, role play, and then provide positive feedback.

Helpful Hints: Select a situation in which a person embarrassed runs away and reacts angrily. Give feedback.

Step 3: Transfer training:

A. **School:** You give a wrong answer to a question.

B. **Home/Community:** You drop a lamp at home.

C. **Peers:** You fall down during a game or make some other mistake.

Comments: What is embarrassment and how does it make you feel? This also would go hand-in-hand with expressing your feelings.

Extended Activities: Puppets. "Dealing with Stress Award," page 120 and "Homework Gram," page 32.

Lesson 40: Handling Embarrassment

1. Am I embarrassed?

2. What caused it?

3. Consider options:

a. Ignore it.

b. Change the topic.

c. Reassure self.

4. Choose an action.

RELIEVING STRESS

Dennis Hanken, Ed.S. and Judith Kennedy, Ed.S.

Lesson 41: Handling Failure

Objective: Students will respond to failure by figuring out why they failed and choosing what to do about it.

Materials Needed: Story, "Three Little Pigs" or optional stories on the following pages.

Establish the Need: Read the "Three Little Pigs" and discuss the wolf's reaction when he could not blow the house down (or a story on the following page). Discuss the first two pigs' houses being blown down.

Procedures:

Step 1: Model the skill:

Model using "Think Aloud" strategies: Reacting to failure in a positive way:

(1) Why did I fail? (lack of effort, skill, luck, etc.) (2) How can I avoid failure in future (practice, try hard, try something else). (3) Try again or try something new.

Step 2: Role play with feedback:

A. In groups of four have your students role play failing at something and using "Think Aloud" strategies for appropriate reaction.

B. More role play practice of appropriate responses.

Helpful Hints: Failing activities could include: (1) Not being able to tie your shoe or ride a bike. (2) Having trouble learning a new concept (writing name, learning math facts, reading). (3) Not being chosen winner of a contest. Have your students role play and react inappropriately for contrast.

Step 3: Transfer training:

A. **School:** Ask the PE teacher to reinforce an appropriate reaction to failure when teaching new skills.

B. **Home/Community:** Tell the parents you are working on handling failure and ask them to reinforce. Be sure the parents understand that you see mistakes as opportunities to learn.

C. **Peers:** What would you do if you failed to get anyone to participate in something you wanted to do?

Comments: It is very important that your students learn the difference between failing at a task and being a failure. Mistakes should be looked at as opportunities to learn.

Extended Activities: Have your students brainstorm as many ways as they can to avoid failure in the future. "Tips for Doing Well on Tests" on page 135. "Dealing with Stress Award," page 120 and "Homework Gram," page 32.

The Class Clown-Fails

Jack, the class clown, loved to have others laugh at him. He often succeeded, but usually got in trouble for it.

There was a very difficult math test on Thursday. Jack studied for it a little, but most of the time he put it off. He thought he could pass it by putting minimal time and effort into studying. On Monday, Ms. Precious gave the math test back to Jack. Well to his surprise he failed the test. Zouch! His parents were very disappointed in him. He thought about his problem for many days. He said to himself, "There is a time to be funny and a time to study. I failed because of lack of effort. The next test I have to try harder and study more. I can't let that one test get me down. I will try a new plan: study and review every day and check my work when done. My parents will be proud of me and I will be proud of myself."

Dear Know It All:

I've got a problem with tests at school. I study the night before a test (or earlier), and I get an "F." I get an "F" on almost every test. My teacher and I are trying to figure out a way that I can remember the stuff for my tests. Do you have any ides on what I could do to remember the stuff?

Dale

Dear Dale,

Feeling nervous about a test is normal. It may sound silly, but studying for a test really begins long before the test. Pay attention in class. The teacher will give you clues about what's going to be on the test. Know the kinds of questions to expect. Will there be multiple choice? T& F? Will you need to know names and dates? Take notes; ask questions.

Don't try to cram everything into one night. Give yourself several review sessions. Study illustrations, maps, graphs. They highlight important people, events, details, facts. Review headings and subheadings. Read the questions at the end of the chapter. Can you answer them? Go over vocabulary words or any italicized words.

Know It All

Tips for Doing Well on Tests

- Go to bed on time the night before and get up in time for a good breakfast.

- Be sure you have all the materials you need-a sharpened pencil, paper, books, notes, maps. Whatever you need.

- Read the directions before starting the test. If you don't understand something, ask your teacher.

- Answer all the questions you know first, leaving ones you are uncertain of until later. However, it is usually best not to go back and change answers, as your first response is often correct.

- Be sure that you answer every question.

- Stay relaxed. If your mind wanders or you feel anxious, breathe deeply.

- Check the clock periodically to make sure you will have enough time to complete the test. Don't hurry. Use the time you need.

- Check your finished paper before handing it in to make sure you answered every item.

- Study a little each day prior to the test, instead of waiting until the last minute.

Lesson 41: Handling Failure

1. Why did I fail?

2. How can I avoid failure in the future?

3. Try again or try something new.

RELIEVING STRESS

Dennis Hanken, Ed.S. and Judith Kennedy, Ed.S.

Lesson 42: Accepting "No"

Objective: Students will be able to accept no without reacting in a negative way.

Materials Needed: Stories, "No Means No" and "A Bad Habit," on the following page.

Establish the Need: Sometimes we will want people to do something or let us do something, and they will say "no." Have your students give some examples of times they were told "no." How did they feel? What did they do?

Procedures:

Step 1: Model the skill:

Demonstrate accepting "no" using "Think Aloud" strategies:

> (1) Why was I told no? (2) What are my choices now? a) Do something else. b) Say how I feel in a friendly way. c) Write or talk about how I feel. (3) Act out my best choice.

Helpful Hints: Elicit feelings that arise when told "no." Brainstorm and write on the board. Brainstorm other choices when told "no."

Step 2: Role play with feedback:

A. Pair your students and have them role play responding to "no" using "Think Aloud" strategies.

B. Your students will practice acceptable ways of reacting to "no." Provide feedback.

Helpful Hints: "No" from an adult may be easier to take than receiving it from one's peers. You students should give a "no" response and another student could react in an inappropriate manner, i.e., stomping off, getting mad, manipulating for contrast.

Step 3: Transfer training:

A. **School:** Your teacher tells you that you can't do an activity. What do you do?

B. **Home/Community:** Your parents say that you cannot stay over at your friend's house. What do you do?

C. **Peers:** A friend tells you that he can't come over because he is busy. What do you do?

Helpful Hints: Accepting "no" is hard for some children. Some may have had parents who did not put many (or put too many) restrictions on the child.

Comments: Saying "no" to someone doesn't mean you don't like them. Sometimes saying "no" is in interest of safety of the other person.

Extended Activities: Story, "Little Red Hen" and how she handled "no" from her friends. Have your students brainstorm activities they can do by themselves at home and at school. "Dealing with Stress Award," page 120 and "Homework Gram," page 32.

No Means No

Johnny, the pushy second grade boy, was always jumping in on games during recess. He always made other children mad by doing this. One day his friends and some other students decided enough was enough. They told him he couldn't play ball with them. He tried to play, but they told him, "No" several times until he got the message. He was totally heartbroken. He never thought people would say "no" to him. I guess his manners were rather poor.

So the next recess, he asked nicely to join the group. The group thought that he deserved a second chance and let him play. He followed the rules and everyone had fun.

Johnny decided from then on to ask and play by the rules. He felt good about himself and was much happier during recess.

A Bad Habit

Tim, a first grader, had difficulty keeping his hands off other boys and girls. At first his friends and classmates thought it was cute, but then they started to dislike it. Finally one of his friends said, "No" when Tim touched him. Tim thought he was just being friendly, but he must be wrong. After that, Tim decided not to touch others just to be friendly.

Lesson 42: Accepting "No"

1. Why was I told no?

2. What are my choices now?

    a. Do something else.

    b. Say how I feel in a friendly way.

    c. Write or talk about how I feel.

3. Act out my best choice.

RELIEVING STRESS

Lesson 43: Saying "No"

Objective: Students will be able to say "no" even if they feel guilty and afraid.

Materials Needed: Chalkboard, puppets.

Establish the Need: Saying "no" is sometimes hard. Help your children brainstorm ideas of when they might say "no" to someone. Help them see that it is okay for them to say "no" even to an adult.

Procedures:

Step 1: Model the skill:

A. Demonstrate to the class saying "no," using puppets and a scenario of one asking the other to do something.

B. Use "Think Aloud" strategies:

> (1) Do I want to do what is asked? (2) Tell the person "no" in a friendly way. (3) Give the reason.

Helpful Hints: Saying "no" requires a risk. Some people have trouble saying "no." Sometimes saying "no" directly to a person is difficult, but you may regret it later if you don't say "no" to something you don't want to do. Discuss "people pleasers."

Step 2: Role play with feedback:

A. Have your students role play saying "no" to another student's request in groups of three. Rotate roles and give feedback to both people. Ask one student to observe and give feedback.

B. More role play saying "no" appropriately.

Helpful Hints: It is very hard for some students to say "no" and it can be a danger to children when asked to do something not in their best interest. This may take considerable practice. Students could say "no" to each other inappropriately for contrast practice.

Step 3: Transfer training:

A. **School:** Friends want you to skip school. What do you do?

B. **Home/Community:** Your brother or sister wants you to watch a particular TV show and you want to watch something else. What do you do?

C. **Peers:** Your friend wants to play a game and you want to go to the mall. What do you do?

Comments: You may want to talk about compromise and what that means.

Extended Activities: You might want to have the counselor in to discuss saying "no" to inappropriate physical touch. "Dealing with Stress Award," page 120 and "Homework Gram," page 32.

Lesson 43: Saying "N0"

1. Do I want to do what is asked?

2. Tell the person "no" in a friendly way.

3. Give the reason.

RELIEVING STRESS

Lesson 44: Relaxing

Objective: Students will use relaxation techniques when needed.

Materials Needed: Tape recorder, music to play that is soothing, the story, "The Sky Is Falling."

Establish the Need: Read "The Sky Is Falling" and discuss how Chicken acted when frightened.

Procedures:

Step 1: Model the skill:

    A. Explain to your students they will handle things better if they are relaxed and not anxious.

    B. Model using "Think Aloud" strategies, the relaxation technique on the following page:

        (1) Do I need to relax? (2) Sit comfortably. (3) Breathe deeply.

Helpful Hints: Discuss ways to tell if body language is anxious. Shoulders tight, shallow breathing, stomach churning.

Step 2: Role play with feedback:

    A. Have your entire class tighten up muscles to see the difference between relaxed and tense. Have them relax. Take your class through the relaxation techniques on the following page.

    B. If a student can catch himself or herself and relax, the results are usually better. Discuss.

    C. More relaxation practice.

Helpful Hints: Soft music helps some people relax. Have a student think of a panic situation. What happens if you don't relax?

Step 3: Transfer training:

    A. **School:** You are about to take an important test, use relaxation techniques.

    B. **Home/Community:** You just had an argument with your brother or sister. Use "Relaxation Technique" on page 143.

    C. **Peers:** You are angry with a friend, but you don't know why. Use relaxation techniques.

Comments: Relaxation techniques are very difficult to learn and will require frequent practice, but have lifelong benefits.

Extended Activities: Take your students through the relaxation techniques before challenging academic tasks. Play soft music when you want the entire group to be calm. "Dealing with Stress Award," page 120 and "Homework Gram," page 32.

Relaxation Technique

- Deep breathing throughout relaxation

- Select a comfortable sitting position.

- Close your eyes, and direct your attention to your own breathing process.

- Think about nothing but your breath, as it flows in and out of your body.

- Say to yourself something like this: "I am relaxing, breathing smoothly and rhythmically. Fresh oxygen flows in and out of my body. I feel calm, renewed and refreshed.

- Continue to focus on your breath as it flows in and out, thinking of nothing but the smooth, rhythmic process of your own breathing.

- After five minutes, stand up, stretch, smile and continue your daily activities.

Educational Media Corporation®, Box 21311, Minneapolis, MN 55421-0311

Lesson 44: Relaxing

1. Do I need to relax?

2. Sit comfortably.

3. Breathe deeply.

RELIEVING STRESS

Lesson 45: Handling Group Pressure

Objective: Students will decide what they want to do when pressured by friends to join in activity.

Materials Needed: Puppets, chalkboard.

Establish the Need: Discuss with your students why people may try to talk them into doing things which aren't in their best interest. List examples.

Procedures:

Step 1: Model the skill:

Model with puppets using "Think Aloud" strategies handling pressure from people asking him or her to do something inappropriate, i.e., tease another child, take something that doesn't belong to me, not telling parents where I'm going. "Think Aloud" strategies:

> (1) What might happen if I do this? (2) Do I want to do this? (3) If I decide no, give a reason. (4) Suggest other things to do.

Step 2: Role play with feedback:

A. Group students in fives and have them take turns trying to talk one student into an inappropriate activity. Rotate the roles and give feedback.

B. Make sure each student practices the role of handling group pressure.

Helpful Hints: Inappropriate activities which could be listed on the board: (1) taking something that belongs to someone else. (2) Not asking permission to use parent's possession. (3) Teasing another child. (4) Not allowing another child to join activity. (5) Calling names. What happens when you do everything that group wants you to do?

Step 3: Transfer training:

A. **School:** Your friend is encouraging you to let him or her copy answers from your paper. What will you do?

B. **Home/Community:** You are at a friend's house. The friend wants you to help him or her get money out of his or her mother's purse. What do you do?

C. **Peers:** The children you are playing with are teasing another child and calling names. What do you do?

Comments: This is a skill which sometimes becomes harder for children as they get older. Now is the time to nurture independence of action.

Extended Activities: (1) Your friends want you to play ball in the street. Your parents have told you not to play in the street. What do you do? (2) You are playing at a friend's house and he or she has some matches. You know it is not safe to play with matches What do you do? "Dealing with Stress Award," page 120 and "Homework Gram," page 32.

Lesson 45: Handling Group Pressure

1. What might happen if I do this?

2. Do I want to do this?

3. If I decide "no," give a reason.

4. Suggest other things to do.

RELIEVING STRESS

Lesson 46: Wanting Other's Possessions

Objective: Students will not take something that belongs to someone else.

Materials Needed: Story "Aladdin's Lamp," chalkboard.

Establish the Need: Read "Aladdin's Lamp" and talk about wanting and taking things that don't belong to us and the possible consequences.

Procedures:

Step 1: Model the skill:

Model using "Think Aloud" strategies: wanting something that isn't mine.

> (1) I want this. (2) Make the best choice: a) Ask to borrow. b) Earn money to buy it. c) Ask to trade. d) Walk away. e) Ask my parents to buy it. (3) Self-reward for not taking it.

Step 2: Role play with feedback:

Establish a scenario: Have your students take turns role playing using "Think Aloud" strategies. Other students can give feedback. Discuss the choices.

Helpful Hints: What happens when you try to keep someone's possessions for a long time? Discuss. Discuss how you would feel if someone took something of yours.

Step 3: Transfer training:

A. **School:** A classmate has a pencil that you really like. What do you do?

B. **Home/Community:** Dad leaves money lying out on his dresser. What do you do?

C. **Peers:** A friend has a game you would like to have. What do you do?

Comments: Stealing is a difficult behavior to stop once it is started, because it is so rewarding if the student isn't caught. You should set up your classroom to minimize opportunities for theft. Having children give themselves positive talk for not stealing is important since only they know when they don't. Encourage statements like, "Good for me, I didn't take it."

Extended Activities: You need a pencil for your seat work, what do you do? You didn't remember to bring your lunch to school, what do you do? Dad left money lying around on the kitchen counter, what do you do? "Dealing with Stress Award," page 120 and "Homework Gram," page 32.

Relieving Stress

Lesson 46: Wanting Other's Possessions

1. I want this.

2. Make the best choice:

    a. Ask to borrow.

    b. Earn money to buy it.

    c. Ask to trade.

    d. Walk away.

    e. Ask my parents to buy it.

3. Self-reward for not taking it.

RELIEVING STRESS

Lesson 47: Knowing When to Tell

Objective: Students will decide when to involve adults in a problem and when to handle it themselves.

Materials Needed: Chalkboard, puppets.

Establish the Need: Using puppets, set up several scenarios contrasting tattling with telling an adult if the situation might hurt someone. (i.e., a child taking a toy from another versus children playing with matches.)

Procedures:

Step 1: Model the skill:

Model how to decide when to get adults involved using "Think Aloud" strategies:

> (1) Will someone get hurt? (2) Whom should I tell? (3) Do it in a friendly way.

Helpful Hints: Help your students understand they need to tell when their own or another's safety is involved. Small children will need a lot of practice.

Step 2: Role play with feedback:

A. Your students will role play knowing when to tell using "Think Aloud" strategies.

B. Have them role play a serious problem on the playground and telling.

Helpful Hints: Have your students role play tattling of a minor problem for contrast.

Step 3: Transfer training:

A. **School:** Someone threatens to hurt you on the playground. What do you do?

B. **Home/Community:** A brother or sister is playing with matches. What do you do?

C. **Peers:** A friend is playing with fire crackers in a garage. What do you do?

Comments: Discuss tattling. Help your students distinguish tattling from telling when they should. Child needs to learn when to involve adult and when to handle it themselves.

Extended Activities: Puppet activities and stories which depict tattling. Have the counselor come in to discuss children needing to tell when someone is hurting them or touching them in ways they don't like. "Dealing with Stress Award," page 120 and "Homework Gram," page 32.

Relieving Stress

Lesson 47: Knowing When To Tell

1. Will someone get hurt?

2. Whom should I tell?

3. Do it in a friendly way.

RELIEVING STRESS

Lesson 48: Wanting to be First

Objective: Students will recognize they cannot always be first.

Materials Needed: Puppets, story "Heather Always Wanted To Be First" on the next page.

Establish the Need: Discuss with your students how they feel when first and how they feel when last. Discuss how impossible it would be for everyone to be first. Use the puppets to demonstrate.

Procedures:

Step 1: Model the skill:

Model the skill using "Think Aloud" strategies: Have several students all try to be first lining up at the door and demonstrate it is an impossibility.

> (1) Not everyone can be first. (2) It's okay not to be first.
> (3) Try hard even if I'm not first.

Helpful Hints: Make sure your students don't get too rough.

Step 2: Role play with feedback:

A. Establish a scenario when a child will be first. Have your students practice "Think Aloud" strategies. Give feedback.

B. Your students share being first and discuss what happens when being first is shared. Give feedback.

Helpful Hints: Scenarios could include: (1) Being picked for a team. (2) Finishing an assignment first. (3) Being first to line up. (4) Being first for show and tell. Discuss for contrast: (Child cannot be first and cries and pouts.)

Step 3: Transfer training:

A. **School:** I want to be first for show and tell. Susie goes first, what do I do?

B. **Home/Community:** I want to be first to play Nintendo. My brother or sister gets to go first, what do I do?

C. **Peers:** I want to get picked first for the playground game. I am not picked first, what do I do?

Comments: Children usually respond if they sense fairness and know they will have their time to be first. Make sure every child has an opportunity to be first and feel special.

Extended Activities: Establish a day or week when one child is your helper and first to line up. Rotate this position. Be sure that every child gets a chance at being first. "Dealing with Stress Award," page 120 and "Homework Gram," page 32.

Heather Always Wanted to be First

Heather was a nice girl in first grade. She seemed to be well liked by the rest of her class, except during group games. She always wanted to be first or have more than one turn. This was even the case when she had to line up or take turns in the class.

Mrs. West took the class out to play hopscotch one day. Of course, Heather was first and then managed to push two girls out of their turn. Mrs. West had Heather take a time out because of her rude behavior. The next day the class went out again, but this time no one picked Heather for their team.

1. Ask your students what lesson the little girl, Heather, needed to learn. Elicit that she needs to learn how to take turns.

2. Ask them to tell how they feel about other people who do not wait to take their turn.

Lesson 48: Wanting to Be First

1. Not everyone can be first.

2. It's okay not to be first.

3. Try hard even if I'm not first.

RELIEVING STRESS

Lesson 49: Determine What Caused the Problem

Objective: Students will be able to recognize what caused the problem and choose an appropriate solution.

Materials Needed: Stories, "DeDe The Talker" and "Peacemaker," on the next page.

Establish the Need: Read "DeDe The Talker." What is the problem? Whose problem is it? What caused the problem? What are some solutions?

Procedures:

Step 1: Model the skill:

A. Model deciding what caused a familiar problem.

B. Demonstrate using "Think Aloud" strategies:

(1) Identify the problem. (2) Is it my problem? (3) What caused it? (4) List choices for solution. (5) Choose.

Helpful Hints: Suggested problems: arguing over who is first in a game or who started the fight, sharing crayons, having a friend mad at you, spilling your milk at lunch.

Step 2: Role play with feedback:

A. Your students will role play a common problem in the class. Decide what the problem is and look for solutions using "Think Aloud" strategies.

B. All students will role play solving recent problem. Talk about identifying the problem, finding a solution, and what caused the problem. Give feedback.

Helpful Hints: Have two students argue over who gets to hand out papers as a contrast activity.

Step 3: Transfer training:

A. **School:** Your classmate will not share the art materials.

B. **Home/Community:** Your friend won't give your bike back.

C. **Peers:** A friend and you have a problem taking turns.

Comments: Center on what is the problem instead of arguing over who did what to whom. Talk about compromising.

Extended Activities: Puppet. "Homework Gram," page 32.

DeDe, The Talker

DeDe, a small third grader, was the gossip queen of her classroom. She talked about anyone and anything to anybody who would listen. Needless to say, she spent a lot of time in the dog house with the teacher. She was not a very good listener, and she blamed everyone else when she got in trouble.

One day her classroom teacher put the students in groups of four for a change of pace from the traditional rows. Well, DeDe was very happy about this because two of her friends were in this group. The teacher explained that all the children had to cooperate with each other and if they did something wrong the whole group might end up paying the consequences. Well, it didn't take long and DeDe had started the talking. The teacher told the group to get together and decide what was the problem and how to solve it. The group decided DeDe's talking had led the group away from their tasks. They had identified the problem. DeDe needs to visit less and the rest of the group needs to ignore DeDe when she visits. DeDe finally agreed she was the main problem. She signed a contract with the group agreeing when it was appropriate to talk. This helped the group cooperate more and get their work done.

Peacemaker

Dear Peacemaker,

I have a problem with my family. We are always yelling at each other. I want my family to be a lot nicer. I hope you will help me.

    Taylor

Dear Taylor,

When you visit a friend, or even a faraway relative, did you ever notice how you put on your best behavior? You try to remember to say "thank you" and "please." You don't grab for the best toy or the biggest piece of pizza. You'd never dream of acting rude. But with your own family... well, it's a different matter.

When people live together day after day, they sometimes begin to take each other-and each other's rights-for granted. Maybe your little brother trashes your room, or your sister borrows your clothes without asking. Your mom has a bad day at work and Dad is tired. Tempers flare and words fly.

There's no easy answer to your problem, Taylor. Ask for a family meeting and talk together about what each of you can do to make things better. Make a list of everyone's suggestions. Then post it in an important place (maybe on the bedroom door). (See next page.)

    Peacemaker

Lesson 49: Determine What Caused the Problem

1. Identify the problem.

2. Is it my problem?

3. What caused it?

4. List choices for solution.

5. Choose.

MAKING DECISIONS

                    Dennis Hanken, Ed.S. and Judith Kennedy, Ed.S.

Lesson 50: Whose Problem is It?

Objective: Students will distinguish between someone else's problem and their own.

Materials Needed: Puppets and chalkboard.

Establish the Need: Use puppets to demonstrate solving one's own problem (like not understanding assignment) and trying to solve someone else's problem (like a friend seems angry with you, but you don't know why).

Procedures:

Step 1: Model the skill:

Using puppets and "Think Aloud" strategies, model distinguishing between when a problem is mine or someone else's. "Think Aloud":

(1) What is the problem? (2) Is it mine or their's? (3) Choose action: a) Solve the problem if mine. b) Offer to help. c) Suggest solutions. d) Leave the person alone.

Step 2: Role play with feedback:

A. Have your students role play in groups of two deciding whose problem it is and what action to take. Rotate and give feedback.

B. Have your students role play a recent problem in the classroom and discuss whose problem is it and work on a solution.

Helpful Hints: It is often difficult for children to realize when a problem is not theirs to solve. Although they should be encouraged to be supportive of a friend with a problem, they need to learn to discriminate whose problem it is. Have your students role play inappropriate responses before going on to more appropriate role playing.

Step 3: Transfer training:

A. **School:** Your friend forgot his or her lunch money. Is this your problem? What do you do?

B. **Home/Community:** Your parents are arguing. Is it your problem? What do you do?

C. **Peers:** Your friend has to move away and is very sad about it. Is it your problem? What do you do?

Comments: This is a subtle, but important skill for children to learn. Many children waste a lot of energy feeling anxiety about a problem that is not theirs to fix and, in fact, is impossible for them to fix.

Extended Activities: When children tattle on other children, it is helpful for them to recognize that this is not their problem to solve. There are many opportunities in a classroom to involve the children in deciding whose problem it is. "Homework Gram," page 32.

Making Decisions

Lesson 50: Whose Problem Is it?

1. What is the problem?

2. Is it mine or their's?

3. Choose action:

   a. Solve the problem if mine.

   b. Offer to help.

   c. Suggest solutions.

   d. Leave the person alone.

MAKING DECISIONS

Lesson 51: Sharing Problems with Others

Objective: Students will recognize the value in sharing problems with others.

Materials Needed: Puppets, tape recorder with taping prior to the lesson.

Establish the Need: Prior to the lesson, have your students record on tapes the problems they would like help with. Discuss: When you have a problem, do you talk it out or hold it inside. Which is better?

Procedures:

Step 1: Model the skill:

Model using "Think Aloud" strategies with puppets (can't understand math assignment, forgot gym shoes or library book, didn't have breakfast today).

(1) What is the problem? (2) Can someone help me? (3) Whom will I tell?

Step 2: Role play with feedback:

A. In groups of 5 or 6, have your students listen to a tape recorded problem and each student offers a solution. The group will pick best solution.

B. Rotate and offer feedback.

C. Lead a discussion on what happens when people do not share their problems.

Helpful Hints: You might need to stress the concept of not discussing the problems with others out on the playground, lunchroom, and so forth. Confidentiality is very important in order for children to feel safe. Establish rule of confidentiality.

Step 3: Transfer training:

A. **School:** You forget your homework at home. What do you do?

B. **Home/Community:** You leave your swimsuit at the pool. What do you do?

C. **Peers:** You want to stay overnight at your friend's house, but his or her mom says no. What do you do?

Comments: Children need not only to learn to share problems with others, but to choose who it is safe to share with. You can model sharing problems appropriately. Some children will have come from families who emphasize keeping secrets. You will need to consider this in working with these children.

Extended Activities: (1) Have class meetings in which your students may seek help with their problems. (2) Have the school counselor or psychologist speak to your class, so the children will know resources for problems that are serious in nature. "Homework Gram," page 32.

Making Decisions

Lesson 51: Sharing Problems with Others

1. What is the problem?

2. Can someone help me?

3. Who will I tell?

MAKING DECISIONS

Dennis Hanken, Ed.S. and Judith Kennedy, Ed.S.

Lesson 52: Accepting Responsibility Versus Blaming Others

Objective: Students will be able to accept responsibility for their actions without blaming others.

Materials Needed: 6 x 18 construction paper, chalkboard.

Establish the Need: Discuss doing something that someone talks you into (stealing, breaking a rule, disobeying parent) which gets you into trouble. Help your students see when it is one's own responsibility for fault. Discuss blaming others for our mistakes.

Procedures:

Step 1: Model the skill:

Model the skill using "Think Aloud" strategies:

(1) Identify the problem (lost a library book). (2) Did I cause it? (3) Choose a response. a) Apologize. b) Replace it. c) Tell the truth.

Step 2: Role play with feedback:

Have your students role play a common problem, decide who caused the problem, and select a correct response. Give feedback.

Helpful Hints: Example: You fail a math test and admit it because you did not study. You fail a math test and you tell your parents it is because the test was not fair.

Step 3: Transfer training:

A. **School:** You forget homework and forget lunch money. Whose responsibility is it?

B. **Home/Community:** You blame sister or brother for starting a fight.

C. **Peers:** Your friend is always teasing you so you call him a name.

Comments: Talk about responsibility. **RESPONSIBILITY**—acknowledging one's own power to choose how to act.

Extended Activities: Give a piece of 6 x 18 construction paper per student and have them divide into four equal sections. Take a problem-a friend accuses you of tattling on him or her to the teacher. Put this in square 1. Square 2, who caused the problem. Square 3, illustrate 2 responses you could make. Square 4, tell which is best response.

Making Decisions

Lesson 52: Accepting Responsibility Versus Blaming Others

1. Identify the problem?

2. Did I cause it?

3. Choose a response.

a. Apologize.

b. Replace it.

c. Tell the truth.

MAKING DECISIONS

Lesson 53: Consequences of Choices and Decisions

Objective: Students will learn that there are consequences for poor choices and decisions.

Materials Needed: Egg, bowl, glass of water, magic marker. Problems on the next page. (Copy on separate index cards.)

Establish the Need: Discuss the decisions of the main characters: in "Snow White" her decision to eat the apple the witch presents, "Hansel & Gretel," their decision to run away from home, "The Three Bears," Goldilocks entering the house of the three bears. Discuss consequences of decisions and other choices characters could have made.

Procedures:

Step 1: Model the skill:

A. Demonstrate cause and effect relationships. (1) Break an egg in a bowl. (2) Tip a glass of water over. (3) Write with a magic marker on cloth.

B. Model using "Think Aloud" strategies making a decision considering its consequence:

(1) What are my choices? (2) What are the likely consequences of each? (3) Pick the best choice.

Step 2: Role play with feedback:

A. Have your students in pairs role play making a decision and knowing its consequence. (List of problems is on page 164.)

B. Have your students role play making decisions for a scenario and choosing the best response. Rotate and give feedback.

Helpful Hints: Your students need to make decisions with an awareness of the consequences involved. Have them demonstrate wrong reaction to being pushed, failing test, missing bus. See the list of problems on the next page.

Step 3: Transfer training:

A. **School:** Someone calls you a name. What do you do?

B. **Home/Community:** Your brother or sister forgot to feed the dog. You get blamed. What do you do?

C. **Peers:** Friend blames you for missing the bus. What are your choices? What do you do?

Comments: Discuss cause and effect. What are the consequences? Define. (What happens as a result of my action? Could be loss of something.)

Extended Activities: (1) Think of something to do that may cause a good or bad thing to happen. (2) Discuss cause and effect. Name a cause and have your students state what might be an effect. (3) Index cards with choices on them. (See activity on the following page. These cards will be used for Lesson 55 also.) "Homework Gram," page 32.

Making Decisions

Direction: Copy the following statements onto separate index cards and have your students brainstorm the possibilities of choices and consequences for each choice.

Cause: Someone calls you a name.

Cause: You disobey the playground supervisor.

Cause: Someone shares his or her dessert with you.

Cause: You give someone a compliment.

Cause: Someone drinks too much soda.

Cause: You stay up late on a school night.

Cause: Someone writes on the bathroom wall with a marker.

Cause: Someone starts a fire playing with matches.

Cause: You help fold the laundry.

Cause: You make your bed without being told.

Cause: You forget to feed your pets.

Cause: You go outside in rain without a coat.

Cause: You wake up late on a school day.

Cause: You forget your homework at home.

Cause: You aren't watching the time and get home late from a friend's house.

Cause: Someone pushes you in the lunch line.

Cause: Someone draws on your desk.

Cause: You forget your lunch money at home.

Cause: You don't do your homework, and it's due today.

Cause: You tell your parent a lie.

Lesson 53: Consequences of Choices and Decisions

1. What are my choices?

2. What are the likely consequences of each?

3. Pick the best choice.

Lesson 54: Differences Between Major and Minor Problems

Objective: Students will be able to distinguish between a minor problem and a major problem and to recognize these perceptions can change.

Materials Needed: Magazines, pictures of people in different situations; a large piece of poster board for every two students, crayons or markers.

Establish the Need: Your students need to know that a major problem needs to be shared with adults and minor problems sometimes can be handled by themselves. If students are unaware of what a major problem is, they might seek help from adults to solve even minor problems. Give examples of minor problems, then major problems. Have your students talk about the problems they need to solve which occur every day. Define a major problem and why they must share that with an adult.

Procedures:

Step 1: Model the skill:

Model distinguishing between major and minor problems using "Think Aloud" strategies:

(1) Gather information. (2) Is this a major or minor problem? a) Major = talk to a safe adult. b) Minor = choose a response. (3) Take responsibility yourself. (4) Try to solve it yourself.

Helpful Hints: Magazines with pictures showing various problem situations. Sometimes what is major for some could be minor for others. New shoes-if specifically made to benefit a disability might be a major problem to the person, but not to others. Consequences can be major and minor too.

Step 2: Role play with feedback:

A. In pairs have your students distinguish whether a problem is major or minor from the pictures you provide.

B. Have your students divide poster board and put picture examples of major problems on one side, minor problems on the other.

Helpful Hints: Have your students react to a minor problem in an inappropriate way. Give feedback.

Step 3: Transfer training:

A. **School:** Decide whether to work hard to get an "A" or not try and get a "D" in social studies.

B. **Home/Community:** Decide on whether to ask your brother or sister to help you fix a bike tire.

C. **Peers:** Decide whether or not to ask your best friend to borrow his or her bike.

Comments: Problems related to school should be discussed. Sometimes social problems are very important to children. Major problems will probably have long-term effects.

Extended Activities: Display magazine pictures on poster board. Create major and minor problems using additional magazine pictures.

Lesson 54: Differences Between Major and Minor Problems

1. Gather information.

2. Is the problem major or minor?

a. Major = talk to a safe adult.

b. Minor = choose a response.

3. Take responsibility yourself.

4. Try to solve it yourself.

MAKING DECISIONS

Lesson 55: Most Problems Have Several Solutions

Objective: Students will come up with at least three solutions for a problem.

Materials Needed: Stories, "Relax, We Can Solve It," or "Being Stubborn," on the next page. Problem cards from Lesson 53.

Establish the Need: Define a problem (a situation which makes you feel bad). You can either do things to make a problem better or worse. Have your students name some problem they can think of. Brainstorm solutions for each. Read "Relax, We Can Solve It" or "Being Stubborn" on the next page.

Procedures:

Step 1: Model the skill:

A. Model using "Think Aloud" strategies, identifying the problem, finding three solutions, implementing one.

B. "Think Aloud":

(1) Take a deep breath and get calm. (2) What is the problem? (3) What are 2 to 3 things I can do about it? (4) Pick the best one for me. (5) Try that one first.

Step 2: Role play with feedback:

A. Distribute problem cards that the students used for Lesson 53. Have them provide three solutions and pick one. Discuss and get feedback.

B. More practice naming three solutions and picking the best one.

Helpful Hints: Have your students name a poor solution to a problem (could be not doing anything).

Step 3: Transfer training:

A. **School:** A teacher calls on you to read or say the alphabet. You don't know where to start.

B. **Home/Community:** You are playing ball with a friend and a kid comes over and takes the ball away.

C. **Peers:** You are playing on the playground when three kids start calling you names and teasing you.

Comments: Help your students see that if one solution doesn't work, they will need to repeat the process.

Extended Activities: "Problem Solving" board game, see Lesson 56. There are innumerable situations that come up in class where you can assist your students in finding more than one solution to a problem. Other school personnel can reinforce this skill too.

Relax, We Can Solve It

It was one of those spring days when everyone was looking forward to playing outside for recess. Mrs. Wonderful's class was having some problems "getting along" in school. Most of the time they couldn't agree on anything in class and seemed to argue over everything.

Mrs. Wonderful decided to have a class meeting and talk about some of the problems. It just so happened the day of the meeting there were several arguments during recess and class time, and everyone seemed a little "mad" at each other.

Mrs. Wonderful said to the group, "Let's all take a couple of deep breaths and maybe we will become calmer." The children tried this and it seemed to help for a couple of minutes. She asked the class what the problem was. John said, "We argue over everything; we can't get along." Mrs. Wonderful said, "Can you tell me three things we could do about it?" The class came up with three things:

> We could be better listeners
>
> We could cooperate more with each other
>
> We could be more considerate of other's feelings

Mrs. Wonderful praised the students for coming up with three solutions. She asked which solution they wanted to try. The class chose number three. She said, "We will try this for a week and see if we argue less." With reminders of their solution, the class began to get along much better.

Being Stubborn

One day Bill, Carl, and Jim got together after school at Bill's house. They were trying to decide what to do that afternoon.

Jim said, "I want to play soccer." "It's too cold," said Carl. "Besides we don't have enough people," Bill said, "I think Carl is right, it is too cold. Why don't we play Nintendo at my house?" "No," Jim said loudly. "I want to play soccer." "We don't want to play soccer," said Carl, "It's too cold." "I don't care," said Jim. "If you won't play soccer, I am going home." "I guess you can go home then," said Bill.

1. Ask your students what other solutions Jim has besides going home?

2. Ask your students how they think Jim will be treated next time the boys get together? Elicit from students that he may not get invited, the other boys won't like him, and he may lose his friends.

Educational Media Corporation®, Box 21311, Minneapolis, MN 55421-0311

Lesson 55: Most Problems Have Several Solutions

1. Take a deep breath and get calm.

2. What is the problem?

3. What are 2 to 3 things I can do about it?

4. Pick the best one for me.

5. Try that one first.

MAKING DECISIONS

Lesson 56: Some Problems Don't Have Good Outcomes

Objective: Students will choose best solution when problem cannot be totally resolved.

Materials Needed: You will need to make materials for "Problem Solving" board game on the following pages.

Establish the Need: Tell your students they are having a birthday party and can invite only six children. You want to invite nine, what do you do?

Procedures:

Step 1: Model the skill:

A. Discuss birthday party invitations showing your students that some problems don't have good solutions.

B. Model using "Think Aloud" strategies solving a problem.

> (1) Breathe deeply and get calm. (2) What is the problem? (3) Think of three solutions. (4) What are the consequences of each? (5) Pick one with the least consequences.

Step 2: Role play with feedback:

A. Put your students in groups of 4 and 6 and have them play the "Problem Solving" board game. Rotate and give feedback.

B. Have your students discuss a current problem at school. Have them name three solutions and choose the best one.

C. Have your students discuss a current problem, but realize that solutions are limited or all somewhat negative.

Step 3: Transfer training:

A. **School:** You need to go to the bathroom, but the teacher said that no one could go during the test.

B. **Home/Community:** Your pet dies and you are very sad. You spend a lot of time thinking about it.

C. **Peers:** Your best friend is moving away in two weeks.

Comments: Children's sense of fairness and black and white reasoning will make it difficult for them to think it is okay to choose what is best in a no-win situation. You will need to support them in this concept.

Extended Activities: Have class discussions to brainstorm solutions to every day problems that come up in the class. Have class meetings to resolve problems your students are experiencing individually or collectively. "Homework Gram," page 32.

Problem Solving Game

Directions: Construct the game board of posterboard or other heavy paper. Use a brass brad in the center to attach the spinner. The students spin the pointer, choose a problem card, and give two to three solutions. Copy the following situations onto separate index cards. Distribute two cards in each space on a game board.

Game Cards

You are accused of stealing money off the teacher's desk. Actually, you know who did it, but don't want to tattle.	You can only invite five kids to your birthday party. There are eight you'd like to have. How do you choose?
Your mom and dad have been arguing a lot lately. They seem unhappy. Your grandma is very worried but doesn't know what's going on. She thinks someone is sick or something. She asks you lots of questions. You don't feel comfortable talking about it.	You are invited to an overnight party, but you're afraid to go because sometimes you walk in your sleep. If you did that at the overnight party, you'd be embarrassed.
Your mom moves out of the house, and you're afraid your parents will get a divorce. You're scared and need someone to talk to.	Your pet rabbit dies. You are very sad and spend all of your time thinking about him and wishing he were alive.
Your dad has been away from home a lot. When he does come home, he has been drinking a lot. There is a lot of yelling. You're scared.	Your best friend is moving away to another town. It bothers you so much, your grades are getting worse.
You have headaches a lot. Your parents take you to the doctor. But now you're worried because, when you asked your mom if you could go to a movie, she said there wasn't enough money. You feel guilty about being sick and having to spend money for the doctor.	You know it is important to tell the truth, but you don't know what to do now. You saw your best friend copy from your paper. If you tell, your friend will get mad.

Dennis Hanken, Ed.S. and Judith Kennedy, Ed.S.

Lesson 56: Some Problems Don't Have Good Outcomes

1. Breathe deeply and get calm.

2. What is the problem?

3. Think of three solutions.

4. What are the consequences of each?

5. Pick one with the least consequences.

MAKING DECISIONS

Lesson 57: Setting Goals and Collecting Data

Objective: Students will be able to set short-term goals and collect sufficient data to make a satisfactory decision.

Materials Needed: Chalkboard, paper, pencils. Reward system for goals reached.

Establish the Need: Goal setting and collecting data are life long skills (even when you buy clothes, choose a movie, choose a friend). Discuss with students why they may need to set goals in their lives.

Procedures:

Step 1: Model the skill:

A. Model using "Think Aloud" strategies, setting a goal.

B. "Think Aloud" strategies:

> (1) What is my goal? (2) What steps do I take? (3) Take the steps one at a time. (4) Reward myself when my goal is reached.

Helpful Hints: You will need to pick an easily achieved goal, such as writing a poem on the board, solving three math problems, and so forth. Define collecting data as gathering necessary information to help me reach my goal.

Step 2: Role play with feedback:

A. In small groups have your students role play choosing a goal using "Think Aloud" strategies. Suggest a goal such as getting a good grade on a test, completing seat work, finding someone to play with.

B. Discuss with your students what happens when a goal isn't reached (repeat process).

C. Your students will set a goal, collect data, follow steps, and then reach their goals. Offer feedback.

Helpful Hints: Things to do before I take a test: Review information ahead of time, don't cram for a test, take a practice test, use "Tips for Doing Well on Tests," Lesson 41.

Step 3: Transfer training:

A. **School:** Set and reach an academic goal in a hard subject for you.

B. **Home/Community:** Set a goal of cleaning your room one day a week.

C. **Peers:** Set a goal of making a new friend.

Comments: Most goals should be short-term for elementary school children. The younger the child the less time between reward and goal. Explain what collecting data means.

Extended Activities: Your students should get into the habit of making goals. Have each student make an academic goal and a social goal each week for nine weeks.

Lesson 57: Setting Goals and Collecting Data

1. What is my goal?

2. What steps do I take?

3. Take the steps one at a time.

4. Reward myself when my goal is reached.

MAKING DECISIONS

Lesson 58: Making the Best Decision

Objective: Students will practice the decision making model.

Materials Needed: None.

Establish the Need: Scenario: I am asked to go swimming with Paul, to a movie with Jim, and on a picnic with Jake, what do I do?

Procedures:

Step 1: Model the skill:

Model making a decision using "Think Aloud" strategies:

(1) What is the situation? (2) Name 2 to 3 decisions I could make. (3) Name the consequences of each. (4) Act on the best decision.

Step 2: Role play with feedback:

A. Introduce a scenario. You are late getting out to recess today. Some kids are playing soccer, some are playing jump rope, some are playing hopscotch. Decide what group you want to join. Your students must follow the "Think Aloud" strategies.

B. Have your students introduce a current problem, use "Think Aloud" strategies and share.

Helpful Hints: See also "Joining In A Group Activity," see Lesson 19. Have a student remember a poor decision. Discuss.

Step 3: Transfer training:

A. **School:** You need to decide whether to do your math first or go to a learning center.

B. **Home/Community:** You get a dollar for raking the lawn. How will you spend the money?

C. **Peers:** Everyone is playing soccer, you want to join in. What do you do?

Comments: Children will need assistance thinking of more than one decision for a situation and consequences attached to each. This may take considerable practice.

Extended Activities: "Homework Gram," page 32.

Lesson 58: Making the Best Decision

1. What is the situation?

2. Name 2 to 3 decisions I could make.

3. Name the Consequences of each.

4. Act on the best decision.

MAKING DECISIONS

Lesson 59: Practicing Self-Control

Objective: Students will be able to use self-control in situations that deal with anger or "out-of-control" behavior.

Materials Needed: Puppets with the story "Ringo Learns to Cool It" on the following pages; book selections under "Extended Activities."

Establish the Need: Being out of control is a natural fear that people have. When you are out of control you can be harmful to yourself and others. Discuss people you have seen with out-of-control behavior. Discuss the consequences. Story: "Ringo Learns To Cool It."

Procedures:

Step 1: Model the skill:

Demonstrate using self-control while having a temper tantrum. "Think Aloud"

> (1) Stop. (2) Take 3 deep breaths. (3) Count to 5. (4) Think about right thing to do. (5) Do the right thing.

Helpful Hints: Talk about body language: feeling sweaty and hot, hands shaking, tone of voice, and so forth.

Step 2: Role play with feedback:

A. Some students role play using self-control when they are mad at friend. Other students should watch and give feedback.

B. Have your students demonstrate being in control after being upset. Give feedback.

Helpful Hints: Possible scenarios: (1) You have the soccer ball, and a boy runs by and takes it. (2) The teacher rips up the paper you worked hard on. (3) A child on the playground calls you a name.

Step 3: Transfer training:

A. **School:** You are several worksheets behind in math.

B. **Home/Community:** Your parents won't let you play after school.

C. **Peers:** A friend takes your bike and has a flat tire.

Comments: See "Relaxing," Lesson 44. If you or others around you can tell that you are losing control, relaxation will be an effective treatment of the situation. Help your students recognize what elicits their loss of control and learn to avoid those situations.

Extended Activities: Book: Sharmot, Marjorie Weinman. *Walter The Wolf.* New York: Holiday House, 1989. Wiseman, Bernard. *Morris and Boris.* New York: Putnam Publishing Group. "Homework Gram," page 32.

Ringo Learns to Cool It

Materials: Three puppets-Ringo, Garth, and Prince.

Have three students volunteer (grades 2 to 3) Grade 1: Have older students come and do the puppet presentation (peer helpers).

Ringo loses control during a game of "Keep Away."

RINGO: Way to go, stupid!! You clutz!

PRINCE: Sorry about that. I didn't mean to hit you with the ball. It was an accident.

RINGO: Well, that certainly is not a good reason. You could have thrown the ball somewhere else. You can never play a game without messing it up.

PRINCE: You are not very nice!!

RINGO: You can never do anything right, Prince. You're just a stupid dude. (Prince leaves the area). Ringo says, "Where are you going? Don't leave!"

Questions for the children:

   What does Prince do?

   Have you ever lost control and hurt somebody's feelings?

Garth tells Ringo that he lost control and hurt Princes' feeling.

GARTH: Howdy, Ringo. What's the problem?

RINGO: Oh! Hi, Garth. What's happening? Have you seen Prince? We want to play "Keep Away" again.

GARTH: Yeah, I saw him standing over in the corner by the fence. But I doubt if he wants to play with you. Start without him.

RINGO: Oh! He probably thinks I am still mad at him, but I got over it.

GARTH: Maybe you ought to think twice before you start calling him names. He won't play with you. You hurt his feelings.

RINGO: He knows I was just blowing off some steam. He'll come back!

GARTH: Just because you are not mad anymore doesn't help, Prince. You were mean and hurt his feelings. Man, you need to gain control of yourself, and when you get mad you can't just call people names. You need to "suck" it up and act your age. Be cool.

Questions for your students:

Is Garth going to come back and play just because Ringo is not mad anymore? (No, his feelings are hurt.)

What was Garth trying to tell Ringo? (When you get upset, try to control your anger.)

RINGO: What do you mean "be cool" or "suck" it up?

GARTH: When you get angry you need to stop, take three deep breaths and think about your choices, and then make the best choice.

RINGO: I thought you are supposed to blow off steam and then forget it.

GARTH: Man, when you're angry, hurting others isn't going to help. You need to find a way to control your anger.

Questions for your students:

Ringo says it's okay to blow off steam and say anything. Is he right? (No.)

What does Ringo need to do? (Learn not to say hurtful things and control his emotions.)

Garth tries to help Ringo learn some other ways to control his anger.

RINGO: What should I do when I get mad?

GARTH: It's okay to get mad, but calling people names and being out of control is wrong and hurtful. You have other choices.

Questions for your students:

Is it wrong for Ringo to get mad? (No.)

What does Ringo need to do different when he is mad? (Use "Think Aloud" strategies.)

Garth helps Ringo make better choices when he is upset or angry.

RINGO: I need to learn to control my emotions when I get angry. Can you help me?

GARTH: When you get angry, the first thing you want to do is stop and think about what you are doing, then take three deep breaths and count to five.

RINGO: What does that do?

GARTH: It helps you to relax and think about your actions and maybe make a good choice about what you're going to do next-you know, instead of calling people names.

Questions for your students:

What is the first step when you feel upset or angry? (Stop and think about what you are doing.)

What is step #2? (Take 3 deep breaths and count to 5.)

Why will these steps help Ringo to have better self-control? (Helps him to relax and focus on making best choice.)

GARTH:	Then after you take 3 deep breaths and count to 5 you think about what the right thing to do is. What should you have done when you were angry with Prince?
RINGO:	Well, he said he didn't mean to hit me with the ball. I should have said something like, "well it was an accident, that's okay and go on playing "Keep Away."
GARTH:	Great! But you kept it up and hurt his feelings. If you would have done the right thing, what would have happened?
RINGO:	Well, we'd still be playing and I wouldn't have hurt his feelings.

Ask your students:

What is the next step after counting to 3? (Think about the right thing to do-like accept the apology and continue the game.

	Ringo apologizes to Prince and hopes he can use the steps next time he gets angry.
RINGO:	What should I do right now?
GARTH:	Well, what are your choices? (1) do nothing, (2) apologize, (3) keep doing the same thing.
RINGO:	Well, I still like Prince, so I should apologize. Hey, Prince!! I am sorry I hurt your feelings. I am going to work on controlling my anger.
PRINCE:	Good idea!!

Questions for your students:

Is this a better way for Ringo to handle his anger? (Yes, and they can still play and be friends.)

Discussion:

Discuss anger and how we need to control it. Everyone gets angry once in awhile and that's okay, but we can't lose control and hurt others.

Replacement Skills

Lesson 59: Practicing Self-Control

1. Stop

2. Take 3 deep breaths.

3. Count to 5.

4. Think about the right thing to do.

5. Do the right thing.

REPLACEMENT SKILLS

Dennis Hanken, Ed.S. and Judith Kennedy, Ed.S.

Lesson 60: Avoiding Poor Choices

Objective: Students will name the consequences of the actions they choose.

Materials Needed: Stories "TJ Changes His Mind" and "Change My Life" on the following page.

Establish the Need: Read the stories and discuss how children could avoid trouble and define consequences. (i.e., consequences are what happens as a result of something you do.)

Procedures:

Step 1: Model the skill:

A. Set up the scenario of avoiding trouble and model using "Think Aloud" strategies:

(1) What are the consequences of the action? (2) What is a good choice and a bad choice? (3) Make the best choice.

B. Discuss the consequences of the decision that would result in trouble.

Step 2: Role play with feedback:

A. Give your students some situations in which they will need to decide to avoid trouble.

B. Have your students in small groups role play avoiding trouble. They need to discuss good choices and poor choices and those consequences. Rotate and give feedback.

Helpful Hints: Your students should discuss consequences of all choices. Possible scenarios: (a) Someone wants you to steal candy at a store. (b) Kids want you to join in teasing others. (c) A friend tries to talk you into doing something your parents said you couldn't. (d) You see money on the table at home.

Step 3: Transfer training:

A. **School:** You and your friends are playing with a bat and ball at recess. A car window gets broken when Sara is up to bat. The teacher asks you what happened.

B. **Home/Community:** Write a note to your parents telling what skill you are on. Ask them to reinforce avoiding trouble.

C. **Peers:** Johnny wants you to walk home with him after school. You try to call home, but the line is busy.

Comments: This is a skill that is connected to various other skills that are integral to helping children be self-responsible and making good choices. It will need considerable practice. (Define the consequences: What is likely to happen as a result of what I do?)

Extended Activities: Brainstorm various situations with difficult solutions. Have your students evaluate which solutions would avoid trouble.

Replacement Skills

TJ Changes His Mind

TJ was a rather large third grader who always seemed to find trouble. In fact, he didn't always have to do anything to be blamed for it.

The month of November was a trying time for TJ. His mother had a baby and he wasn't getting much attention at home. It seemed everything he did at school was wrong. His self-concept seemed really low.

One day he received about four assignments that were due on Friday. He didn't like doing any of them. So he got mad at the teacher and decided not to do them. Well, on Thursday he got really nervous and thought he was going to be in big trouble with the teacher and his parents. First, he thought, "I will have to stay after school and do them anyway. My parents will ground me and I'll be miserable." So he got to work right after school on Thursday and worked till bedtime. He did get them done, but why wait until the last minute? Whew!" "I avoided those consequences. I feel much better about myself. I even like my new brother even though he gets all the attention, but that will change! I have to remember that I have choices. I think I made a good decision. I think I'll do homework sooner, it's not worth it putting it off to the last minute and not planning ahead."

Change My Life

Dear Mr. Change My Life,

I have a problem about lying and cheating. And I want to stop!

   Steve

Dear Steve,

Do you know the hardest thing about changing your behavior? Admitting you need to change. And you've already done that!

Have you ever tried to break a bad habit? Maybe biting your nails or watching too much TV? It's not easy! Habits become habits because you do them over and over and over-until you just do them without thinking. Maybe lying and cheating are becoming like that for you. And you need to stop now. The longer you wait, the harder it will be.

Nothing good ever comes from dishonesty, Steve. And it makes you feel miserable, doesn't it? That churning inside you is your conscience-sort of a built-in radar system to steer you away from doing wrong.

Do you need to make some new friends? Ask to sit somewhere else at school? Talk to an adult you trust? Whatever you need to do, do it!

   Change My Life

Lesson 60: Avoiding Poor Choices

1. What are the consequences of the action?

2. What is a good choice and a bad choice?

3. Make the best choice.

REPLACEMENT SKILLS

Lesson 61: Avoiding Fights

Objective: Students will avoid fights by practicing other ways to handle aggression.

Materials Needed: Puppets, book, *My Name Is Not Dummy*

Establish the Need: Read *My Name Is Not Dummy* by Elizabeth Crary or the puppet story, "Outlaw Avoids a Fight," on the following pages.

Procedures:

Step 1: Model the skill:

A. Model using "Think Aloud" strategies avoiding fights:

(1) Stop! (2) Choose: a) Walk away. b) Resolve the problem by talking. c) Ask someone to help with the problem. d) Yell for help and run away.

B. Discuss the consequences of fighting.

C. Discuss the positives of not fighting. Help your students see there are other choices.

Step 2: Role play with feedback:

A. Using the puppets, have your students role play avoiding fights. Other students can assist you to evaluate and give feedback.

B. Discuss what happens when people fight. What are the feelings?

C. Discuss a problem that resulted in a nonphysical fight. What were other solutions?

Helpful Hints: Possible scenarios: (1) Some students call you names. (2) A boy threatens to beat you up. (3) Some kids push you toward a dog on a chain. (4) Someone takes your money away.

Step 3: Transfer training:

A. **School:** Another student has been taking your lunch away every day.

B. **Home/Community:** A child pushes you off your bike and takes the bike.

C. **Peers:** When you go to the bathroom, a group of kids come in and threatens you.

Comments: Handling aggression is part of every child's life and is a crucial skill to learn.

Extended Activities: Practice assertive training. Your school psychologist has materials on this. Books: Cosgrove, Stephen *Hucklebug*. Los Angeles: Price Stern Sloan, Inc. 1978. Keats, Ezra Jack. *Goggles*. New York: McMillian, 1978. "Homework Gram," page 32.

Outlaw Avoids a Flight

Materials: Three puppets-Outlaw, Desperado, Sheriff

Need three volunteers or puppets (grades 2 to 3). You need peer helpers from the upper grades or other adults to help out for grade 1.

OUTLAW: I love to just lay around, but it's getting kind of hot. I better find some shade. I need a nice spot. Oh!! That's a perfect place.

DESPERADO: Hey, this is my place, first come and it's mine, all mine.

OUTLAW: I believe I spotted it first.

DESPERADO: Give it a rest, man. This is my place. You want to fight about it?

OUTLAW: Whatever! You think you're just going to take this place without a struggle?

DESPERADO: Hey, this means war. What will it be guns, fists, wrestling, rocks?

Questions for your students:

What is the main problem between the two? (They both want the same spot.)

Are they trying to compromise or trying to get the best of each other? (Fighting to see who is the best.)

OUTLAW: You know something. This isn't worth it, I think I'll leave and go to town and look for something fun to do.

DESPERADO: Pardon me!! I thought you wanted to fight.

OUTLAW: And hurt this face, NAW! I'd rather go look for some fun. (Pause)

(He goes silently out the back door while Desperado is putting his mean look on and getting ready to fight.)

DESPERADO: Hey, where did he go?

SHERIFF: Hey, mister Outlaw, what's your hurry?

OUTLAW: Well, I am in a hurry. I decided not to fight that Desperado and not get into trouble.

SHERIFF: Good idea. You're getting smarter with age. You know it takes a better person to stop and count to 5, ignore, or walk away from a fight. Besides, I never saw fighting accomplish anything.

Questions for your students:

Should you walk away from fights or fight to settle an argument or whatever you're fighting about?

Is walking away a good idea?

SHERIFF: You may be an Outlaw, but if someone is "bugging" you, you can try to ignore them. If that doesn't work, you might as well leave, walk away. It just isn't worth fighting. Someone gets hurt or you end up in trouble.

OUTLAW: Some people just want to fight about everything no matter what. They're desperate for attention.

Questions for your students:

When should you ignore people? (When they are "bugging" you or trying to get you mad.)

Is it okay to walk away from someone when you are upset with them. (Sure, and sometimes the sooner the better.)

OUTLAW: Thanks Sheriff! I need to do this more often and change my image.

SHERIFF: By the way, I know a place where you can go and have fun without getting into a fight.

OUTLAW: Sounds great!

Questions for your students:

What steps did the Sheriff suggest to Outlaw for avoiding fights?

Stop and count to 5.

Decide on choice:

Walk away.

Talk to the person to try to resolve problem.

Ask someone to help solve problem.

Yell for help and run away.

Discuss:

What happens if problems occur when you can't walk away, like in class or during lunch?

When does an adult help in these situations? Also talk about why tattling is such a problem with some kids. Talk about situations that have happened to them where they had to stop and count, walk away, and so forth.

Lesson 61: Avoiding Fights

1. Stop.

2. Choose:

a. Walk away.

b. Resolve the problem by talking.

c. Ask someone to help with the problem.

d. Yell for help and run away.

REPLACEMENT SKILLS

Lesson 62: Expressing Your Anger

Objective: Students will express anger without hitting.

Materials Needed: Book, *A Terrible Thing That Happened At Our House* by Marg Blaine. Puppets. Alternate book, *Angry* by Susan Riley.

Establish the Need: Read the book and talk about anger: feeling angry is okay, what we do with our anger is what matters.

Procedures:

Step 1: Model the skill:

With puppets, model expressing anger using "Think Aloud" strategies:

> (1) Stop and count to 5. (2) Why am I angry? (3) Choose: a) Tell a person. b) Walk away. c) Take three breaths. (4) Write about how I feel. (5) Problem-solve, (see Lesson 49).

Step 2: Role play with feedback:

A. Put your students in groups of three and have them rotate role playing expressing anger with one evaluator. Rotate and provide feedback.

B. More role playing expressing anger appropriately using "Think Aloud" strategies.

Helpful Hints: Suggested scenarios: (1) Your friend talks about you behind your back. (2) Your teacher treats you unfairly. (3) You get blamed for something you didn't do. (4) Your parents won't let you stay overnight at friends. (5) You forgot your homework at home and are angry with yourself. (6) A classmate hits you with a pencil while tossing it to someone else. Your students role play inappropriate expressions of anger for contrast.

Step 3: Transfer training:

A. **School:** Your teacher makes you stay in at recess to finish your seat work.

B. **Home/Community:** You are watching a TV show and your dad comes in and changes the channel.

C. **Peers:** Your friend said he or she would play with you, but now he or she is playing with someone else instead.

Comments: Writing out or drawing angry feelings is good for children who internalize angry feelings and are not good at verbalizing.

Extended Activities: Your students can put on plays which depict appropriate expressions of anger. Hitting, kicking, pushing, shoving, poking, and pinching are not acceptable. Books: *Walter, The Wolf* by Margorie Weinman Sharmat, *Morris Borris* by Bernard Wiseman and *I Can't Wait* by Elizabeth Crary. "Homework Gram," page 32.

Lesson 62: Expressing Your Anger

1. Stop and count to 5.

2. Why am I angry?

3. Choose:

a. Tell a person.

b. Walk away.

c. Take three breath.

4. Write about how I feel.

5. Problem-solve.

REPLACEMENT SKILLS

Lesson 63: Relating to Another's Anger

Objective: Students will listen to another's anger and choose a response.

Materials Needed: Choice of books (see below), puppets.

Establish the Need: Read an appropriate story (*I Can't Wait, I Want It, I Want To Play* or *My Name Is Not Dummy* by Elizabeth Crary or *Little Mouse On The Prairie*, Stephen Cosgrove).

Procedures:

Step 1: Model the skill:

Model using "Think Aloud" strategies, responding to another's anger:

> (1) Listen to the person's concern. (2) Choose: a) Keep listening. b) Ask why the person is angry. c) Suggest a solution. d) Walk away. e) Ask for help.

Step 2: Role play with feedback:

A. Give your students role playing ideas and have them role play by two's in front of the class with you and your students offering feedback.

B. Role play appropriate relating to anger using "Think Aloud" strategies.

Helpful Hints: Suggested scenarios: (1) Your friend is angry because you didn't ask him or her to play your game. (2) Your teacher is angry with you for being out of your seat. (3) You mom is mad at you for spilling juice on the rug. (4) Your brother is mad at you for going in his room. Have some pairs of students role play inappropriate relating to another's anger. Discuss.

Step 3: Transfer training:

A. **School:** Your teacher is angry with you for doing poorly on a test.

B. **Home/Community:** Your parents are angry with you for not coming in the house on time.

C. **Peers:** Your friend is mad at you for losing his or her ball.

Comments: This is a difficult task even for adults and will require considerable practice for some children.

Extended Activities: Discuss being victimized by bullies or adults and the need to tell someone and ask for help. Counselors are good resources for activities with this. "Homework Gram," page 32.

Lesson 63: Relating to Another's Anger

1. Listen to the person's concern.

2. Choose:

a. Keep listening.

b. Ask why the person is angry.

c. Suggest a solution.

d. Walk away.

e. Ask for help!

REPLACEMENT SKILLS

Lesson 64: Responding to Accusations

Objective: Students will respond to an accusation by choosing to honestly deny, explain, or apologize for their behavior.

Materials Needed: Chalkboard and homework.

Establish the Need: Lead your students in a discussion about being accused of something they did or did not do. How did they respond? How do they feel about their response?

Procedures:

Step 1: Model the skill:

Model using "Think Aloud" strategies being accused of something:

(1) Is the accusation correct? (2) Decide on a response. (3) Think of an honest response. a) Say, "I didn't do it." b) Agree, "I did it." c) Apologize. d) Fix the problem.

Step 2: Role play with feedback:

A. In pairs, your students will role play responding to an accusation using "Think Aloud" strategies. Rotate and give feedback.

B. More role play on an appropriate response to accusations.

Helpful Hints: Your students might role play responding inappropriately to accusations for contrast.

Step 3: Transfer training:

A. **School:** A teacher has accused you of stealing.

B. **Home/Community:** Your parents accuse you of breaking a window next door.

C. **Peers:** A friend accuses you of ruining his new tape.

Comments: Accusations can have a damaging effect on a person's well being. Emphasize to your students to be sure before accusing anyone of wrong doing. Honesty should also be emphasized, and the need to admit wrong doing and correct, if possible.

Extended Activities: Puppets and stories that incorporate being accused. "Homework Gram," page 32. "Alice in Wonderland" has examples.

Lesson 64: Responding to Accusations

1. Is the accusation correct?

2. Decide on a response.

3. Think of an honest response:

a. Say, "I didn't do it."

b. Agree, "I did it."

c. Apologize.

d. Fix the problem.

REPLACEMENT SKILLS

Lesson 65: Negotiating

Objective: Students will use negotiating skills when there is a conflict.

Materials Needed: Puppets.

Establish the Need: Puppets fight over a toy and whose turn it is to have the toy. Puppets with the story, "Sharing A Skate Board Causes A Problem" on the following pages.

Procedures:

Step 1: Model the skill:

Using "Think Aloud" strategies, model negotiating skills:

(1) State the problem. (2) Say what I want. (3) Listen to the other person. (4) Make a plan. (5) Follow the plan.

Step 2: Role play with feedback:

A. Group your students in small groups, and give them suggested situations to role play. Rotate and give feedback.

B. Your students should discuss what happens when you can't agree or reach consensus.

C. Negotiate a current problem using "Think Aloud" strategies. Discuss.

Helpful Hints: Suggested situations: (1) You and another student both want the same book at free time. (2) You are coloring, and your brother/sister wants to model. There is only one table to use. (3) Everyone wants to be first to line up for recess. (4) Everyone wants to hold the puppy brought to class. (5) You and your partner both want to use the blue marker.

Step 3: Transfer training:

A. **School:** Your teacher wants you to do math and you want to go to the Learning Center.

B. **Home/Community:** Your parents want to watch one TV show and you want to watch another.

C. **Peers:** Your friend wants to ride a bike and you want to play a game.

Comments: Negotiating and compromising are high level skills. You should use every opportunity to develop, practice, and reinforce this skill.

Extended Activities: Have a class meeting where your students present ideas for change. Use negotiating skills. "Problem Solving Game," see Lesson 56. Book: Cosgrove, Stephen. *Little Mouse on the Prairie.* Los Angeles: Price Stern Sloan Inc., 1978.

Sharing a Skate Board Causes a Problem

Materials: Three puppets-Goofy, Bugsy, Whinnie. Ask for volunteers from grades 2 to 3 for grade 1. Have peer helpers or older students for volunteers.

Goofy and Bugsy buy a skate board together.

GOOFY:	Wow! Look at that skate board. I'd like to have that.
BUGSY:	Yeah! But look at the price. Neither one of us can afford that.
GOOFY:	True, but if we pool our money and each pay half, we could buy it and share it 50/50.
BUGSY:	Great idea!! Lets do it!
GOOFY:	What a great board, did you see me jump that curb?
BUGSY:	My turn-hey you already had two extra turns.
GOOFY:	Get a life! I need to use it more because I am better.
BUGSY:	This isn't fair, you said 50/50.
GOOFY:	I didn't mean exactly 50/50. Quit griping.
WHINNIE:	You guys should be enjoying the skate board instead of arguing all the time.

Questions for your students:

What is the main problem with Goofy and Bugsy? (Can't share, argue.)

How do they try to solve the problem? (Arguing.)

How should they try to solve the problem? (Compromise, share 50/50.)

Whinnie helps Bugsy and Goofy make a plan.

BUGSY:	Goofy, you want it all to yourself, but half of it is mine.
GOOFY:	You are a whiner! You'll get your turn. I just need to use it more because I am so good.
WHINNIE:	You two could argue all day and never have any fun. You both need to have a written plan so you quit arguing.
GOOFY:	A written plan?
BUGSY:	What do you mean a plan?
WHINNIE:	You need to sit down and write up a way to solve your problem.
BUGSY:	Are you crazy? We don't have a problem. It's all Goofy's problem. He doesn't want to share 50/50.
GOOFY:	You complain about everything. It's no big deal!

WHINNIE:	You guys can't even agree about anything. No wonder you can't share the board. See why you need a plan?
GOOFY:	I guess you're right. What next?
WHINNIE:	First you decide what is the problem. Then you decide what you are going to do. Listen to the other person, then you are ready to make a plan.

Questions for your students:

What are the first three steps? (Look at "Think Aloud" strategies.)

GOOFY:	We definitely know what the problem is-sharing the skate board.
BUGSY:	You got that right. 50/50.
GOOFY:	It can't always be exactly 50/50. What do you want to do, use a stop watch?
WHINNIE:	Well, what is your plan? You can't argue about every detail. Compromise might work.
GOOFY:	Okay! Why don't we use the board in certain areas and we can't take extra turns.
BUGSY:	We can always use the same run which is about the same time. That seems fair.

Questions for your students:

What is the fourth step? (Decide on plan.)

What was Whinnie's suggestion to Bugsy and Goofy? (Compromise.)

BUGSY:	There's a place we could use! It's your turn.
GOOFY:	Thanks! So if we agree on the place and take turns, don't argue about the time, we should be okay. I'll write this down just to make sure.
WHINNIE:	That sounds like a great plan. You did a good job of negotiating.
GOOFY:	What's that word mean?
WHINNIE:	Negotiate is like a compromise. You try to solve a problem by listening and talking and then come up with a plan.

Questions for your students:

Do compromise and negotiate have the same meaning? (Yes.)

What does negotiating mean? (Talking together and coming up with a fair plan.)

GOOFY:　　　Oh, who's turn is it? I am ready to have fun and quit arguing.

BUGSY:　　　Amen! Lets get with it!

Lets review the steps for negotiating:

    State the problem.

    Say what I want.

    Listen to other person.

    Make a plan.

    Follow the plan.

Discuss negotiating; how it means to "give in a little." Also talk about compromising/cooperation.

Lesson 65: Negotiating

1. State the problem.

2. Say what I want.

3. Listen to the other person.

4. Make a plan.

5. Follow the plan.

REPLACEMENT SKILLS

Lesson 66: Overreacting

Objective: Students will name and choose options to a problem after relaxing.

Materials Needed: Relaxation techniques, see Lesson 44. The story, "The Sky is Falling."

Establish the Need: Some time we overreact to a situation because we are in a bad mood, ill, or in a hurry. Discuss how you feel after you overreact. Discuss the Hen's over reaction to events making her think the sky is falling.

Procedures:

Step 1: Model the skill:

A. Model overreacting to a situation, i.e., not finding a book, losing a pen. Discuss.

B. Model using "Think Aloud" strategies not overreacting:

> (1) Name the problem. (2) Give three solutions. (3) Name the worst thing that could happen. (4) What would I do then? (5) Implement the best solution.

Step 2: Role play with feedback:

A. Lead relaxation techniques. Put your students in small groups and give them suggested situations. Students take turns role playing and evaluating. Rotate and give feedback.

B. Have your students pick a problem and then use the techniques. Discuss reaction.

Helpful Hints: Suggested strategies: (1) You leave your lunch or homework at home. (2) Your best friend does not want to play with you at recess. (3) You want to play videos and your friend wants to ride bike. (4) Kids call you names. (5) You want to go on a picnic, but it is raining. (6) You want to ride your bike, but it has a flat tire. (7) You did your worksheet wrong and have to redo it. Over react to someone cutting in line or stepping on your toe. Discuss contrast of body sensations and feelings.

Step 3: Transfer training:

A. **School:** You did the wrong page of the workbook.

B. **Home/Community:** You and your dad were going fishing, but now he has to work instead.

C. **Peers:** You were going to stay overnight at a friend's, but he got sick.

Comments: It is important to have children, especially "worriers" name the worst thing that can happen because it is usually not as bad as it seems.

Extended Activities: Watch the movie, *Winnie The Pooh,* and discuss Eeyore's woeful approach to situations. Have children discuss other choices Eeyore can make. Read "The Princess and the Pea" and discuss her overreacting and discuss the consequences. "Homework Gram," page 32.

Lesson 66: Overreacting

1. Name the problem.

2. Give three solutions.

3. Name the worst thing that could happen.

4. What would I do then?

5. Implement the best solution.

REPLACEMENT SKILLS

Lesson 67: Recognizing What Makes You Lose Control

Objective: Students will be able to recognize what makes them lose control and regain control.

Materials Needed: Chalkboard, paper, pencils, posters.

Establish the Need: If you can recognize what makes you lose control, then you are better able to control yourself. Discuss with your students things that can be very upsetting and the consequences of losing control (getting hurt or hurting someone, breaking something, making a poor choice for oneself).

Procedures:

Step 1: Model the skill:

Model using "Think Aloud" strategies things that can upset a person.

> (1) What really upsets me? (2) List those things. (3) What do I do when I'm upset? (4) What can I do instead?

Helpful Hints: With your students' help, make a list of things that are really upsetting. Talk about body posture and tone of voice.

Step 2: Role play with feedback:

A. In groups of three students, role play using "Think Aloud" strategies.

B. Discuss why a situation makes you react a certain way.

C. Go over the list and see if you can eliminate any areas that are upsetting.

D. Discuss inappropriate things to do when a person is upset.

Helpful Hints: Discuss with your students that some people seem to know how to "push our buttons"-(make us more upset than we want to be). Help your students see that they do choose their reactions. Discuss other ways to handle things when upset.

Step 3: Transfer training:

A. **School:** What makes you lose control at school (adults, stress, grades)?

B. **Home/Community:** What makes you lose control at home (brother/sister, parents, dog, neighbors)?

C. **Peers:** What makes you lose control with a friend (being bossy, name calling, teasing, breaking a promise)?

Comments: What does lose control mean? This relates to major and minor problems.

Extended Activities: The counselors have some excellent materials on this and could be invited to come to class to share. Master "Homework Gram," page 32.

Lesson 67: Recognizing What Makes You Lose Control

1. What really upsets me?

2. List those things.

3. What do I do when I'm upset?

4. What can I do instead?

REPLACEMENT SKILLS

Lesson 68: Deciding If It's Fair

Objective: Students will be able to distinguish if situations are fair and respond appropriately.

Materials Needed: None.

Establish the Need: Children feel more comfortable talking about feelings if they operate in a fair environment. Discuss how it feels when you think certain students get all the attention or seem to be teacher's pet. Stories, "Fanny Fair" and "Raising My Hand," on the next page.

Procedures:

Step 1: Model the skill:

A. Model deciding if it's fair and how people feel when situations aren't fair.

B. What can I do when things aren't fair?

C. "Think Aloud" strategies:

>(1) Am I being treated equally? (2) What can I do to change the situation?

Helpful Hints: This could be a good time to discuss what accommodations people with disabilities need to help them have a fair chance.

Step 2: Role play with feedback:

A. Your students will demonstrate what to do if they feel situations are not fair. Give feedback.

B. Your students will react negatively to unfairness. Give feedback.

C. Have your students demonstrate deciding if it is fair and responding politely. Give feedback.

Step 3: Transfer training:

A. **School:** Your teacher picks the same students to run errands for him or her.

B. **Home/Community:** Both you and your sister or brother want to watch different TV shows. Your parents pick your sibling's choice.

C. **Peers:** You want to let another friend play, but the child you're playing with doesn't want the other friend to play. What do you do?

Comments: Discuss what being fair means? Maybe the person who created the unfairness doesn't really think about the situation or another's feelings.

Extended Activities: Puppets. Life offers enumerable opportunities to determine fairness and to choose one's response to unfair treatment.

Replacement Skills

Fanny Fair

Fanny did a lot of complaining about things not being fair. She often complained to her parents that her brother and sisters got more attention and clothes than she did. She complained to the teacher that she never got to pass out papers or be the leader in class. She complained to her friends about being left out in games. Fanny spent most of her time complaining and not always looking at other's view points. She mostly thought about herself.

One day in school the PE teacher told Fanny and Fred that they could pick teams for softball. First Fanny picked then Fred. Fanny complained and moaned about Fred getting the good players. So Fred gave in and Fanny ended up with the good players, but none of her friends. After class all her friends complained to Fanny that all she wanted to do was win and she wasn't being fair. Her friends wouldn't talk to her until she apologized. Fanny finally realized what it was like to be accused of not being fair. She apologized to her friends. From that time on she looked at situations from others' view before she even mentioned the word "fair." She also took appropriate action by deciding what she could do to change the situation when she or others were treated unfairly.

Raising My Hand

Every time I raise my hand in science class, the teacher calls on someone else. I wonder why? Maybe I talk to much or raise my hand too much and don't let others talk. You know how I love science—I just can't stop talking about it; but, it's not fair to exclude others. You know the teacher is trying to be fair and include others. I guess every time is kind of an exaggeration. Anyway and I'll just try to be patient.

Lesson 68: Deciding If It's Fair

1. Am I being treated fairly?

2. What can I do to change it?

REPLACEMENT SKILLS

Lesson 69: Everyone is Different

Objective: Students will name qualities and characteristics of self and others that make them unique.

Materials Needed: Students, pencils.

Establish the Need: Have your students examine their own pencils carefully for special characteristics that would help identify them. Put all pencils in a pile. Have your students find their own pencils. Discuss how each student found his or her own pencil. What if the students had been in a pile; how would you find each one?

Procedures:

Step 1: Model the skill:

Model naming your own different qualities and characteristics using "Think Aloud" strategies:

(1) What makes me different from other people? (2) What things do I do well?

Helpful Hints: You may need to emphasize keeping the remarks in a positive vein.

Step 2: Role play with feedback:

Divide your students into small groups. Each student takes a turn telling special characteristics of himself or herself with group assistance. Rotate and give feedback.

Helpful Hints: Your students could also name positive characteristics of others in group.

Step 3: Transfer training:

A. **School:** Draw a picture of yourself and name all your special characteristics.

B. **Home/Community:** Inform your parents of the unit you are working on and ask them to reinforce positive attributes of their children.

C. **Peers:** Pair your students. Each student must say something positive about self and the other taking turns. (3 minutes)

Comments: Many incidences will have happened in some children's lives to negatively impact their self-esteem. Your classroom is a wonderful place to help rebuild damaged self-concepts.

Extended Activities: Have your students stand in a circle with a ball of yarn, say positive statement to another person and toss the ball of yarn to that person (holding on to end of yarn). Continue until yarn is used. (Point is to show interconnectedness and promote uniqueness of each person).

Self Acceptance

Lesson 69: Everyone is Different

1. What makes me different from other people?

2. What things I do well?

SELF-ACCEPTANCE

Lesson 70: What are My Strengths and Weaknesses?

Objective: Students will be able to recognize their strengths and weaknesses.

Materials Needed: Paper and pencils, chalkboard.

Establish the Need: Discuss your strengths and weaknesses. Are they the same as others see in you? Is it easier to talk about your strengths or weaknesses?

Procedures:

Step 1: Model the skill:

A. List your strengths and weaknesses.

B. "Think Aloud" strategies:

(1) What do I do well? (2) What areas can I improve?

Helpful Hints: Some students will have trouble listing any strengths and will need support.

Step 2: Role play with feedback:

A. Each student goes to the center of the room. Other students say strengths about this person.

B. Each student lists five weaknesses and ten strengths on paper or verbally.

Step 3: Transfer training:

A. **School:** Ask your principal to come to class. Each student tells the principal one personal strength.

B. **Home/Community:** At the dinner table take turns telling each other what you like about them.

C. **Peers:** Tell your best friend why you like him or her so much.

Comments: To be a good friend, you accept yourself and the other person with his or her strengths and weaknesses. Emphasize that all people can do some things well while other things are harder. Nobody can do everything perfectly.

Extended Activities: Every student gets to have people say positive things about himself or herself. "Accomplished/Still Learning Chart" on the next page.

Accomplished/Still Learning Chart

Directions: Reproduce the chart below on a large sheet of poster paper and have each student complete it.

	Accomplished	Still Learning
Cut out shapes	_____	_____
Write your name	_____	_____
Write ABC's	_____	_____
Ride a bike	_____	_____
Jump rope	_____	_____
Count to 50	_____	_____
Play the violin	_____	_____
Speak more than one language	_____	_____
Swim	_____	_____
Sing 2 songs	_____	_____
Be a good friend	_____	_____
Have a pet	_____	_____
Read	_____	_____

Lesson 70: What are My Strengths and Weaknesses

1. What do I do well?

2. What can I improve?

SELF-ACCEPTANCE

Lesson 71: How is Being Unique Important?

Objective: Students will learn each person has different qualities which make him or her unique.

Materials Needed: "Find Someone Who" game on the next page.

Establish the Need: Do the "Find Someone Who" game.

Procedures:

Step 1: Model the skill:

A. Explain you are handing out charts that they will complete by walking quietly around class and filling in the name of a classmate who has that characteristic.

B. Rules of the game: (1) no talking, (2) no running, (3) no shoving, (4) use a student's name only once.

C. "Think Aloud" strategies:

> What do I have that no one else has?

Step 2: Role play with feedback:

Divide your students into small groups and discuss what each child has that no one else has. Rotate and give feedback.

Helpful Hints: Ideas for different: (1) missing tooth, (2) darkest hair, (3) hide in smallest place, (4) tallest, (5) wear glasses, (6) has lived somewhere else, (7) has no jewelry, (8) wearing jeans. Role play being different. What do people say about you? Discuss.

Step 3: Transfer training:

A. **School:** Tell the school staff what skill your class is working on and ask them to acknowledge your students' differences in a positive way.

B. **Home/Community:** Tell your class how your family is different.

C. **Peers:** Do you know anyone unique in your neighborhood? Class discussion.

Comments: This is a good way to introduce your students to children of other races and cultures and/or children with disabilities and to appreciate their uniqueness and what each has to offer.

Extended Activities: (1) Students list favorite things and compare to see how unique each is. (2) Make an "All About Me" poster. Have the students draw, use photos, or cut pictures and make a collage showing different things they like to do. Hang these posters in the class so your students can see and discuss. (3) Have people of different ethnic backgrounds come to class to discuss their culture and how difference is valuable. (4) Have your students list all of the things about themselves that are different. Celebrate the differences. Use each student's quality of being different to enhance the class.

Self Acceptance

Find Someone Who

Directions: Make this chart large enough so that names can be written in as students find people with these qualities. Only use a name one time.

Is wearing green	Is missing two teeth	Lives on same street since birth
Loves to sing	Rides a bike	Has traveled out of state
Has lived in a foreign country	Likes math	Has three pets
Has grandparents in this city	Has one brother	Rides a horse
Plays a musical instrument	Goes camping	Has lived in three states
Wears glasses	Likes popcorn	Is new to the school

                                           Dennis Hanken, Ed.S. and Judith Kennedy, Ed.S.

Lesson 72: Recognizing How People Change

Objective: Students will be able to recognize how they have changed in the last 1 to 2 years.

Materials Needed: Chalkboard, students will need pictures or objects from past.

Establish the Need: As you physically grow older, you do change in looks and in the way you act. Can criminals change? Have you changed in the last year in physical form or in personality? Discuss. Elicit from your students how they have changed since being a baby. Display an old photo of yourself that shows a change in your appearance. Discuss the changes.

Procedures:

Step 1: Model the skill:

A. Demonstrate what you were like before being a teacher.

B. "Think Aloud" strategies:

(1) How was I as a baby? (2) As a toddler? (3) Now?

Helpful Hints: Changing is part of life. There are good and bad things about growing older. Can you stop from changing?

Step 2: Role play with feedback:

Bring pictures and objects to school from your past and talk about how you have changed. Discuss.

Helpful Hints: Can you name people who try not to change? Name changes you like and dislike.

Step 3: Transfer training:

A. **School:** Why do you think you do different, more difficult things in each grade?

B. **Home/Community:** Do your parents treat you different from how they did two years ago?

C. **Peers:** You have had a friend who is no longer your best friend. What happened? Did you or friend change?

Comments: If people didn't change, what kind of world would it be?

Extended Activities: Have your students bring an object to school to show that they have changed since they played with this before. Bring pictures of them two to three years ago. Make a display of the photos. How has your school, city, or town changed?

Lesson 72: Recognizing How People Change

1. How was I as a baby?

2. As a toddler?

3. Now?

SELF-ACCEPTANCE

Dennis Hanken, Ed.S. and Judith Kennedy, Ed.S.

Lesson 73: It's Normal to Make Mistakes

Objective: Students learn that everyone makes mistakes and that is natural.

Materials Needed: Story on the following page.

Establish the Need: Read the story on the next page.

Procedures:

Step 1: Model the skill:

A. Model by giving an example of a mistake you made and what you learned. Ask your students if they ever made a mistake. How did they feel about the mistake? Use self disclosure to discuss your own mistakes.

B. "Think Aloud" strategies:

(1) Did I do something wrong? (2) Was it my fault? (3) What can I learn from the mistake?

Step 2: Role play with feedback:

A. Have three volunteers try to juggle three tennis balls without making a mistake. Discuss.

B. Discuss how we can learn by our mistakes.

Step 3: Transfer training:

A. **School:** Alert the staff to the skill being taught and ask them to reinforce your students learning from mistakes.

B. **Home/Community:** Write a letter to the parents explaining the lesson and ask them to reinforce your students learning from mistakes.

C. **Peers:** Give examples to your class and ask for suggestions on what a child should do: (1) Jeff did wrong page for math assignment. (2) Susie left her bike out and it was taken. (3) Beth carried koolaid into the living room and spilled it on the carpet.

Comments: Students who have trouble mastering academic tasks are at particular risk for having good self-concepts. It is very important to help them set attainable goals and praise them for what they have accomplished.

Extended Activities: You might consider grading all papers in class by marking those right to demonstrate mistakes are okay and not the focus of the class.

Self Acceptance

The Grape Juice Story

Jeff was watching TV while pouring himself some grape juice. He didn't realize that his glass was full, and the purple liquid ran all over his mother's new chair covers.

"Oh, boy," said Jeff. "Is Mom ever going to be mad at me."

He tried to wipe it up with a wet cloth, but the water just spread the purple juice further.

Questions for your students:

What was Jeff's mistake?

What can he learn from it?

What might he do now and in the future?

Lesson 73: It's Normal to Make Mistakes

1. Did I do something wrong?

2. Was it my fault?

3. What can I learn from the mistake?

SELF-ACCEPTANCE

Lesson 74: It's Not Necessary for Everyone to Like You

Objective: Students will discuss that not everyone will like them, but they are still okay.

Materials Needed: Puppets (3).

Establish the Need: Discuss how you feel when you think someone doesn't like you. Do you act differently? The same? Why?

Procedures:

Step 1: Model the skill:

A. Model using puppets having one puppet expressing not liking another. The puppet who is confronted with this verbalizes he or she is okay using "Think Aloud" strategies:

> (1) Does the person have good reason to not like me? (2) Do I want to change the way I act? (3) What is my choice?

B. Model some interactions with people you know.

Step 2: Role play with feedback:

Your students can role play with puppets having one puppet not liking another.

Helpful Hints: This is a difficult task for children with a poor self-identity or who have been trained to be "people pleasers."

Step 3: Transfer training:

A. **School:** The teacher is always calling on you. Sometimes you think your teacher is "picking" on you or doesn't like you.

B. **Home/Community:** Your brother or sister can't seem to say anything nice about you.

C. **Peers:** Your friend plays with you after school, but never during recess.

Comments: It is helpful for children to make a positive list about themselves.

Extended Activities: Do a sociogram of your class to see who is well accepted and who is not. Ask for help from the counselor or psychologist to help an unaccepted child make friends. Help your students see that sometimes they will want to change self-defeating behavior.

Lesson 74: It's Not Necessary for Everyone to Like You

1. Does the person have good reason to not like me?

2. Do I want to change?

3. What is my choice?

SELF-ACCEPTANCE

Lesson 75: Self Put Downs are Damaging

Objective: Student will experience difference between put downs in self-talk and positive self-talk.

Materials Needed: Two puppets to demonstrate the difference between negative and positive self-talk.

Establish the Need: Use puppets to demonstrate the difference between negative self-talk and positive. Ask your students which they think makes a person feel better.

Procedures:

Step 1: Model the skill:

A. Explain that negative self-talk can affect the way we think about ourselves as much or more than positive self-talk can.

B. Elicit from your students some negative self-talk, i.e., write on board. Draw an X through each negative comment.

C. Model positive self-talk.

D. "Think Aloud" strategies:

(1) How do I talk to myself? (2) Tell myself three good things about me.

Helpful Hints: Help your students see the difference between positive self-talk and bragging.

Step 2: Role play with feedback:

A. Assign your students to small groups and have them practice positive self-talk. Each child has a turn while other students evaluate and give support. Rotate and give feedback.

Step 3: Transfer training:

A. **School:** A student draws a picture or writes a positive self statement and says to self each morning.

B. **Home/Community:** Ask the parents to help their students to come up with a statement at home to say daily for positive self-talk.

C. **Peers:** Ask your students to make a contract with another student to make positive statements and support each other in them.

Comments: Self-affirmations are very valuable and will benefit your students. Ideas for content are: (I am likable, I am honest, I am a hard worker, I am attractive, I do math well.

Extended Activities: (1) In small groups have your students rotate role of saying a positive self-statement. You might also include positive statement of another. (2) Reinforce examples of positive self-talk in your class while gently, but firmly, not allowing any put-down talk.

Lesson 75: Self Put Downs are Damaging

1. How do I talk to myself?

2. Tell myself three good things about me.

SELF-ACCEPTANCE

Lesson 76: Are You What People Say?

Objective: Students will be able to recognize the difference between what people think about them and how they see themselves.

Materials Needed: Four copies of the story, "Getting Glasses," on the next page.

Establish the Need: People can be very cruel and the things they say about you may not be true. How do you feel when people say things about you which are not true? Discuss.

Procedures:

Step 1: Model the skill:

A. Model sorting out what some people might say about you versus how you see yourself.

B. "Think Aloud" strategies:

"Am I what other people say?"

Step 2: Role play with feedback:

A. Assign the handout, you need four volunteers to role play the different parts.

B. Discuss and give feedback.

Helpful Hints: Most people are sensitive to being called names and being teased. Children will often do more teasing if they get a reaction.

Step 3: Transfer training:

A. **School:** Two classmates are talking about you and you overhear the conversation.

B. **Home/Community:** Your brother or sister can't say anything nice to you.

C. **Peers:** Your friend tells another child you don't like him or her when it isn't true.

Comments: Help your students to feel good about themselves, so that inevitable teasing has less effect.

Extended Activities: Puppets. Read "Cinderella" and discuss what the stepmother and stepsisters said about Cinderella versus how Cinderella saw herself.

Getting Glasses

The scene: Walking to school. Child #1 has just gotten glasses.

Child #2:	Walks across street, notices child #1's glasses, and points them out to friends, child #3 and #4.
Child #1:	Starts talking to the friend he is walking with.
Child #2:	Walks over to Child #1 and calls him "four eyes."
Child #3:	Laughs and says to Child #1, "Hey, blind as-a-bat, what are you doin'?"
Child #1:	Just sits there and doesn't say anything.
Child #4:	Announces in a loud voice, "Hey, everybody! Here's four eyes. If anyone needs a seeing eye dog, he knows where to get it!"
Child #1:	Starts talking again to the friend he is sitting with.
Child #2:	Says loudly to his friends, "Hey, he better watch out or he'll trip over his feet cause he can't see them."
Child #1:	Getting irritated, but he says to his friend, "It won't do any good to get mad at them. I know I'm not "four eyes," so I'm not going to let what they say bother me."

Lesson 76: Are You What People Say?

Am I what other people say?

SELF-ACCEPTANCE

         Dennis Hanken, Ed.S. and Judith Kennedy, Ed.S.

Lesson 77: Trying or Doing Your Best

Objective: Students will experience trying and doing their best even when they don't succeed.

Materials Needed: Books for students to balance on their heads.

Establish the Need: Have your students try things which will be hard for them such as balancing a book on their heads while they walk. Discuss with your students how they felt by trying, how they felt when they failed, and when they succeeded.

Procedures:

Step 1: Model the skill:

A. Model using "Think Aloud" strategies trying to do a task that you cannot, such as balancing a pencil vertically on your finger. Have fun with it.

B. "Think Aloud" strategies:

(1) What is the task? (2) Can I do it? (3) What will happen if I try? (4) Try my best.

C. Discuss why you are glad you tried even though you failed.

Step 2: Role play with feedback:

A. Pair your students and have them role play trying something hard and doing their best using "Think Aloud" strategies. It could be balancing on one foot.

B. Rotate and give feedback. You could use worksheets, physical tasks, or games as activities.

Helpful Hints: Have your students role play not trying. Discuss how many things would not have been discovered if people hadn't tried.

Step 3: Transfer training:

A. **School:** Ask the PE teacher to reinforce the skill of trying to do your best.

B. **Home/Community:** Write a note home to the parents and ask them to reinforce their children when they do their best on tasks such as making beds.

C. **Peers:** Report to your class something that you tried to do your best on at home over the weekend.

Comments: Your students need to learn that it is okay to try something, even if it is hard and even if they can't do it immediately.

Extended Activities: Reward your students for trying in the classroom. Also reward them for doing their best on a daily basis.

Lesson 77: Trying or
Doing Your Best

1. What is the task?

2. Can I do it?

3. What will happen if I try?

4. Try my best.

SELF-ACCEPTANCE

Bibliography

Periodical

Fleming, D.C., Ritchie, B., & Fleming, E.R. (Spring, 1983). "Fostering the Social Adjustment of Disturbed Students." Teaching *Exceptional Children,* 172-175.

Gresham, F.M. (February, 1982). "Misguided Mainstreaming: The Case for Social Skills Training with Handicapped Children." *Exceptional Children,* 422-431.

Pekarik, E.G., Prinz, R.J., & Weintraub, D.E., Sheldon, & Neale, J.M. (1976). "A Sociometric Technique for Assessing Children's Social Behavior." *Journal of Abnormal Child Psychology,* 4, 1, 83-97.

Rutherford, Robert B. (July, 1997). "Why Doesn't Social Skills Training Work?" *Council for Exceptional Children,* 14.

Books

Aesop. (1993). *Aesop's fables.* New York: Grosset & Dunlap.

Bellack, A.S., & Morrison, R.L. (1982). "Interpersonal Dysfunction" in *International handbook of behavior modification and therapy.* New York & London: Penum Press., 717-743.

Brockman, M.P. (1985). "Best Practices in Assessment of Social Skills and Peer Interaction" in *Best practices in school psychology.* Kent, OH: National Association of School Psychologists, 43-609.

Frank, R.A., & Edwards, P.P. (1993). *Building self-esteem.* Portland, OR: Ednick Communications.

Cartledge, G., & Fellows Milburn, J. (1986). *Teaching social skills to children.* Needham Heights, MA: Allyn & Bacon.

Gresham, F.M. "Best Practice in Social Skills Training" in *Best practices in school psychology.* Kent, OH: National Association of School Psychologists, 181-192.

Huggins, P., Wood Manion, D., & Moen, L. (1993). *Teaching friendship skills: Intermediate version.* Longmont, CO: Sopris West.

Madaras, L. (1993). *My feelings, my self.* New York: Newmarket.

McCarney, S.B. (1989). *Attention deficit disorders intervention manual.* Columbia, MO: Hawthorne.

McGinnis, E., & Goldstein, A.P. (1984). *Skillstreaming the elementary school child.* Champaign, IL: Research.

Rich, D. (1992). *Megaskills.* New York: Houghton Mifflin.

Vernon, A. (1989). *Thinking, feeling, and behaving.* Champaign, IL: Research.

DATE DUE

Demco, Inc. 38-293

Dennis Hanken, Ed.S. and Judith Kennedy, Ed.S.